100 Years'

of the

2nd Batt. West India Regiment

From Date of Raising 1795 to 1898

Compiled by
Colonel J. E. Caulfield

The Naval & Military Press Ltd

Published by
The Naval & Military Press Ltd
Unit 10, Ridgewood Industrial Park,
Uckfield, East Sussex,
TN22 5QE England
Tel: +44 (0) 1825 749494
Fax: +44 (0) 1825 765701
www.naval-military-press.com

In reprinting in facsimile from the original, any imperfections are inevitably reproduced and the quality may fall short of modern type and cartographic standards.

Printed and bound by Antony Rowe Ltd, Eastbourne

Centenary Centre Piece 1795—1895.

100 Years' History

of the

2nd West India Regiment.

LONDON:
FORSTER GROOM & Co.,
15, Charing Cross, S.W.

List of the Senior Lieutenant-Colonels of the 2nd West India Regiment who have Commanded the Regiment or Battalion, with their dates as Lieut.-Colonel in the Regiment.

NAME.	Date as Lieut.-Colonel in the Regiment.
Samuel Graham	20th May, 1795.
Hugh Lyle Carmichael .	18th January, 1797
Sir Benjamin D'Urban, K.C.B. .	7th January, 1808.
Alexander Maclean . .	1st April, 1813.
John Grey Ross . . .	29th June, 1815.
Thomas Bradley . .	16th March, 1820.
Edward Burke . . .	24th August, 1820.
Edward O'Hara . . .	2nd May, 1822.
William Sutherland . .	16th May, 1822.
Thomas Craig . . .	25th June, 1824.
Norman McLeod . . .	30th April, 1827.
Alex. Wolfe Macdonald .	18th October, 1827.
Sir Francis Cockburn . .	30th July, 1829.
Henry C. Cobbe . . .	26th May, 1844.
Stephen John Hill . . .	6th January, 1854.
Henry Wase Whitfeild .	3rd February, 1854.
William Hill	13th August, 1868.
James Delamain Mends .	28th October, 1868.
Robert W. Harley, C.B. . .	7th May, 1870.
Horatio J. Wise . . .	23rd April, 1871.
George D. Webber, C.B. . .	19th October, 1872.

Lionel L. Brett . . .	31st October, 1877.
Sir William O. Lanyon, K.C.M.G., C.B.	2nd February, 1878.
Robert Straker Turton . .	2nd February, 1878.
Ponsonby Sheppard . .	1st January, 1883.
Commanding Regiment .	2nd February, 1883.
Thomas Talbot . . .	2nd February, 1883.
Commanding Regiment .	2nd February, 1887.
William G. Patchett .	2nd February, 1887.
Commanding Regiment .	29th June, 1887.
John M. Maltby . . .	29th January, 1888.
Commanding Battalion .	29th June, 1891.
James E. W. S. Caulfeild .	29th June, 1891.
Commanding Battalion .	24th February, 1892.

PREFACE.

The following history of the 2nd West India Regiment from date of raising (1795) to present year 1895 has been taken from various sources by me.

The late Colonel Ellis left some notes from which it was evident that it was his intention if he had lived to have compiled a history—this helped me very much as far as the first five years were concerned.

The Digest of Service of the 2nd West India Regiment, although very incomplete, was of considerable assistance to me.

Colonel Ellis's History of the 1st West India Regiment gave me much information on many points where the two regiments were on service together.

H.E. Mr. Llewelyn, Governor of the Gambia, was good enough to assist me with regard to the Sabaggee Expedition.

The Secretary of State for War was also good enough to give me certain information—and finally from the old Order Books, Letter Books, Returns, &c., filed in the Brigade Office, belonging to Gambia, Sierra Leone, Gold Coast and Lagos—I was fortunate enough to collect a vast amount of valuable and reliable information.

I hope that my work may be the means of making the officers better acquainted with the excellent past records of their corps, and by so doing, keep alive that *espirit de corps* so essential to the well-being of a regiment.

J. E. CAULFEILD, *Colonel.*

Commanding 2nd W.I. Regiment.

SIERRA LEONE,

April 3rd, 1896.

100 YEARS' HISTORY

OF THE

2ND WEST INDIA REGIMENT.

CHAPTER I.

1793. **Introduction.**

On the declaration of war against Great Britain by the French on 1st February, 1793, an Armament was despatched to the West Indies in November, 1793, under Sir Charles Grey, and although the British were successful in Martinique, Guadaloupe and St. Lucia, it was found in 1794 that more troops were required to garrison these islands.

1794. **Carib revolt in St. Vincent.**

At St. Vincent the Caribs revolted on the 10th March, 1795, and were joined by the French planters of republican sympathies, the Militia were called out and attacked the enemy, but were repulsed with loss.

The Caribs flushed with success, advanced against Kingstown the capital of the island taking up a strong position. On the 13th March the enemy were attacked (at midnight) by a force of Militia, Volunteers, trustworthy negroes, a company of 46th Regiment, and some Seamen

1795. and Marines from the " Zebra," and succeeded in routing them.

The gallant behaviour of the negroes on this occasion induced the Governor (Colonel Seaton) to raise a black corps.

Raising of the St. Vincent Rangers.

Raising 2nd W. I. Regt. by drafts from St. Vincent Rangers.

Brigadier-General Myers appointed Colonel.

For this purpose, free blacks and slaves purchased from the planters, were enrolled into a corps entitled the "St. Vincent Rangers." The letters of service raising the regiment was dated 24th April, 1795, on which date it was taken upon the establishment of the British Army, receiving no pay from the island. Colonel William Myers was appointed from the 15th Foot to be Colonel (in the *London Gazette* of 2nd May, 1795) to date from 24th April, the Regiment being then styled " 2nd West India Regiment," or "Myers' Regiment of Foot," and was composed of drafts from the St. Vincent Rangers.

Lieut.-Colonel Graham to command.

Samuel Graham was appointed Lieut.-Colonel.

At first the establishment of the Regiment was nine (9) companies of infantry and one (1) troop of cavalry, but the scheme of having cavalry as a portion of the establishment was abandoned in 1797. The new regiment was stationed at Martinique until September, when it was moved to St. Vincent.

The following Officers were serving in 1795 :—

RANK.	NAME.	REGIMENT.	ARMY.
Colonel.	WILLIAM MYERS (Br.-Gnl.)	24th Apl., 1795.	1st March, 1795.
Lt.-Col.	SAMUEL GRAHAM.	20th May, ,,	
Major.	WILLIAM HUTCHINSON.	,, ,, ,,	
Captn.	WILLIAM GORDON.	1st July, ,,	1st March, 1794.
,, (c)	THOMAS HUXLEY.	,, ,, ,,	19th Decr., 1793.
,,	MURDOCH MCLEAN.	,, ,, ,,	
,,	JAMES CUMINE.	,, ,, ,,	
,,	ANDREW THOMPSON.	,, ,, ,,	
,,	RICHD. GERALD ELRINGTON.	,, ,, ,,	
,,	BERY WYNNE OTLEY.	,, ,, ,,	
,,	SAMUEL BROWN.	,, ,, ,,	
,,	EDWARD WILLIAMSON.	1st Octbr., ,,	
,,	WILLIAM LYSTER.	16th Dec., ,,	24th Nov., 1793.
Lieut.	LEWIS GRANT.	1st July, ,,	15th Feb., 1794.
,,	J. SANKEY DARLEY.	,, ,, ,,	24th Sept., ,,
,,	RICHARD AINSWORTH.	,, ,, ,,	11th Octr., ,,
,,	R. ROSS ROWAN.	,, ,, ,,	12th Nov., ,,
,,	WILLIAM POTTER.	,, ,, ,,	15th Nov., ,,
,,	ADAM MCPHERSON.	,, ,, ,,	
,,	JOHN ROSS.	,, ,, ,,	
,,	WILLIAM DRUMMOND.	,, ,, ,,	
,,	JOHN GRIFFITH.	,, ,, ,,	
,, (c)	JOHN WHYTE.	,, ,, ,,	
,,	FRANCIS EDMINSTONE.	,, ,, ,,	
,, (c)	J. STAINES.	9th Septr., ,,	
Ensign	RICHARD SMYTH,	1st July, ,,	
,,	HENRY HARDING.	,, ,, ,,	
,,	CHARLES MAXWELL.	,, ,, ,,	
,,	MATHEW JOWES.	,, ,, ,,	
,,	LAWRENCE ARNOTT.	,, ,, ,,	
,,	JOHN BRYAN.	,, ,, ,,	
,,	W. MCDONALD.	,, ,, ,,	
,,	H. BURNS.	,, ,, ,,	
,,	T. DYHES.	,, ,, ,,	

Ensign	M. PARSONS.	1st July, 1795.
,,	DONALD CAMPBELL.	,, ,, ,,
(Cornet)	JOHN MARTIN.	,, ,, ,,
,,	JOHN MALCOLM.	,, ,, ,,
,,	HENRY VAUGHAN.	,, ,, ,,
,,	JOHN CAMPBELL.	,, ,, ,,
,,	WILLIAM REDDING.	,, ,, ,,
Adjt.	WILLIAM MOORE.	,, ,, ,,
Qr.-Mr.	JAMES FLAGHERTY.	,, ,, ,,
Surgeon	J. MITCHELL.	18th Nov., ,,

1795.

St. Vincent Rangers amalgamated into 2nd W.I. Regt.

On the 10th October, 1795, the St. Vincent Rangers, 247 strong was drafted into the "2nd West India, of Brig. Genl. Myers' Regiment of Foot," which prior to that date consisted only of 15 sergeants, 9 drummers, and 84 rank and file, and the St. Vincent Rangers ceased to exist by that name.

In the March 1796 Army List we find the following among the eight regiments headed "Regiments raised to serve in the West Indies."

"Myers' Regiment of Foot formerly the St. Vincent Rangers."

ERRATA.

Page 16, Chap. III., marginal note Granada *read* Grenada.
,, 16, ,, line 10 ,, ,, ,,
,, 17, ,, margin ,, ,, ,,
,, 18, ,, ,, twice ,, ,, ,,
,, 18, ,, line 16 ,, ,, ,,
,, 19, ,, 5 *delete* one West.
,, 21, ,, 2 Leward *read* Leeward.
,, 22, ,, bottom of page, Ansterdam *read* Amsterdam.
,, 23, ,, 2nd paragraph ,, ,, ,,
,, 27, ,, line 5, Villeuneve *read* Villenueve.
,, 32, Chap. IV., line 20, *delete one* on.

Chapter II.

1796. At the beginning of the year 1796, the Caribs were still acting on the offensive.

St. Vincent. Action of Calonery.

Brigadier-General Steward in a despatch writes as follows :—

" About 3 a.m. on the 8th instant (January, " 1796) the enemy made an attack on our left " where we had a three-pounder and cohort " placed upon a tongue of land which ran out " about 50 yards, thought from the steepness on " each side to be almost inaccessible. On the " first shot I immediately ran out as fast as the " darkness would permit me. I found the men all " paraded and Brigadier-General Strutt who had " just received a wound in the face, exerting him- " self much with the 54th Regiment.

" I still proceeded to the left, but from the " darkness could not distinguish the enemy from " our own soldiers (about this time a French " officer who had got over our works was taken " prisoner) and not being certain whether the " enemy had taken possession of the battery on " our left, I directed Major Harcourt to reinforce " that post with a picquet of the 40th, but before " this could be done I had too much reason to " believe it was taken, and immediately despatched " a message to Lieut.-Colonel Graham to bring up

1796. "the whole or part of the 2nd West India "Regiment, but before the message had got many "yards, a firing was heard on the right from the "enemy, and all along the front: I was proceeding "to the right to see what was going on there, when "I heard that the battery I had left had been "taken.

"At this time the troops in front and right of "the line gave way, and the enemy took possession "of the remaining battery. In this dilemna "nothing but a retreat could be thought of."

The rout was indeed complete—nothing was saved—guns and stores were all abandoned to the enemy. Fortunately, Lieut.-Colonel Graham had on the morning of the 7th moved with the 2nd West India, about 200 strong, from Beabon towards the scene of action, and at the time the camp was attacked was only about a mile away. He at once advanced to cover the retreat. This was effected with some difficulty, as the enemy hung about the right and rear, harassing the flight by occupying the different ridges which commanded the road. However, although the 2nd West India suffered severely, they succeeded in keeping the enemy in check until the fugitives had reached Beabon. The total British loss on this occasion was nearly 400 of all ranks, of which the 2nd West India lost no less than 152, or over three-fourths (¾) of the men brought into action.

The troops halted a few hours at Beabon, but that place being 12 miles from Kingstown and destitute of supplies, they retired to that place.

It was now necessary to abandon all the distant posts, the remaining troops being concentrated for the defence of Kingstown and positions round it. A strong position was taken up at Millar's

1796. Ridge, the new Vegie and Morne roads being abandoned. The enemy, advancing as the British retired, took up a position opposite and caused much annoyance by the use of some mortars they had captured. It was therefore determined to attempt the recapture of these mortars, and on the 20th January before daybreak, a body of 250 men, including a detachment 2nd West India, led by Lieut.-Colonel Prevost, endeavoured to surprise the enemy, who, however, were too strong to be dislodged; and the British, their commander being twice wounded, were obliged to fall back. Encouraged by their success, the enemy in their turn became the assailants, advancing at daybreak against Millar's Ridge, and continuing their attacks with great vigour throughout the day, finally retired at night-fall to their original position. The British loss was nearly 60, of which the 2nd West India lost 8 killed and 10 wounded. The relative positions of the contending forces remained practically *in statu quo* until the 8th June, 1796, on which date Sir Ralph Abercromby was able to land a considerable force at Kingstown, and on the morning of the 10th, attacked the enemy, who had now concentrated their forces on the Vegie, turning their left flank.

St. Vincent. Carib War. Action of Millar's Ridge.

1796. Attack and Assault on Vegie.

With considerable difficulty, two 12-pounders, two 6-pounders and two howitzers were advanced to within 600 yards and opened fire at 7 a.m. on the enemy's works, but still they kept their position, and at 2 p.m. it became necessary to order an assault.

A part of Lowenstien's Corps, two (2) companies 42nd, and a detachment of the Island Rangers availing themselves of the profile of the hill, occupied a position within a very short distance of the redoubts. Two (2) more companies of the 42nd, with the "Buffs" and York Rangers,

1796. being ordered up, the assault was successfully carried out, and the enemy retired to the New Vegie, now completely surrounded, and cut off from the Carib Country, but holding, at the same time, a strong position.

Coke, Vol. 2, page 245, says—"That on

1796. "the 18th June, a detachment 2nd West India, "under Lieut.-Colonel Graham, having pursued

Action on Colonarie River "the line formed by the bed of the Colonarie "River to a considerable elevation, discovered a "large party of the enemy strongly fortified; they "invited him to approach with the utmost seeming "sincerity of friendship, which he did at the head "of his men, displaying a white handkerchief in "his hand, indicative of his pacific disposition, "but when he had got within a few yards of their "works, a whole volley of musketry was poured "around him, which killed an officer of Sateur's "corps, and badly wounded the Colonel and "many others—our troops carried off the wounded "and retreated."

Lieut.-Colonel Dickson, 34th Regt., was now ordered to make a diversion with the remains of his own and the 2nd West India, which succeeded beyond expectation, the Caribs being forced to abandon their posts, 700 laying down their arms as prisoners of war; the British loss in this action being about 200, of which the 2nd West India lost as follows:—

Loss in Action. Killed—Captain McLean and one (1) sergeant; wounded—Captain Elrington and nine (9) rank and file.

Although the enemy were now practically broken up and disorganised, they still continued to give trouble.

1796.
St. Vincent.
Carib War.

The following extract from the Historical Record of the 42nd gives an idea of the duty on which the Regiment was at this time employed—

" On one occasion two parties of the 42nd " and one of the 2nd West India were ordered " out, each taking a different direction. The par- " ties of the 42nd attacked the posts and drove the " enemy further into the woods; the soldiers of the " 2nd West India were also engaged, and had " several men killed and wounded.

" The outposts being frequently alarmed by " parties of the enemy firing at the sentries at " night, a sergeant and 12 Highlanders under " Lieut. David Steward penetrated into the woods " at 9 o'clock in the evening with short swords, to " cut their way through the underwood to discover " the post or camp from whence these nightly " alarms came. After traversing the woods all " night an open spot with a sentry was discovered. " This man fired his musket at a dog which ac- " companied the soldiers, and then plunged into " the wood, as the sergeant ran forward to cut him " down. The soldiers were at the edge of a " perpendicular precipice of great depth, at the " bottom of which was seen a small valley crowded " with huts from whence issued swarms of people, " on hearing the report of their sentry's musket.

" Having made this discovery the soldiers " commenced their journey back, but when they " were about halfway, they were assailed by a fire " of musketry on both flanks and in the rear. The " Caribs were expert climbers, every tree appeared " to be manned in an instant: the wood was in a " blaze but not a man was to be seen, the enemy " being concealed by thick and luxuriant foliage.

" As the Highlanders retreated, firing from

1796. St. Vincent. Carib War.

" time to time at the spot from whence the enemy's " fire proceeded, the Caribs followed with as much " rapidity as if they had sprung from tree to tree " like monkeys; in this manner the retreat was " continued until the men got clear of the woods. " The Highlanders were met by a party of the 2nd " West India, sent to their support under Lieut. " Jowes, who was wounded. The loss on this " occasion was six (6) killed and eight (8) wounded " belonging to both corps."

By the middle of October, 1796, the majority of the Caribs had surrendered, and by the end of that month the island was entirely pacified, the Caribs being removed to the Isle of Rattan, in the Bay of Honduras.

St. Vincent. End of Carib War.

The return of killed and wounded during period 20th July to 15th October, 1797, for the 2nd West India is as follows :—

Killed: one (1) sergeant, four (4) rank and file; wounded: Lieut.-Colonel Graham, Ensign Jowes, and three (3) rank and file.

The following letter is an honourable testimony of the services of the corps from the General in command:

" November 16th, 1796.

" SIR,

" I beg you, the officers, and soldiers of the " 2nd West India Regiment, under your com- " mand, will be pleased to accept of my best " thanks for the zeal and activity and humanity " which have been testified by you and them upon " all occasions whilst under my command during

1796.
St. Vincent.

"the Brigand and Carib War in the Island of St. "Vincent.

" I have, &c.,
" (Signed) P. HUNTER, M.-General.
"To
" Captain THOMPSON,
" Commanding 2nd W.I. Regt."

Captain Thompson was presented with a sword of honour by the inhabitants, and Lieut. Porter was thanked in public orders by Major-General Hunter for a gallant and successful attack upon a strong post of the enemy.

A sergeant was also "liberally rewarded" at the same time "in approbation of his brave "conduct on that occasion."

The Regiment suffered so severely from losses in action and from fatigue during the campaign that in April, 1797, it had only an effective strength of 143 privates.

The following table appears in the regimental pay list for period from 25th June to 24th December, 1796:

Ranks.	Colonel	Lt.-Col.	Majors	Capts.	Lieuts.	Ensigns	Adjt.	Surgeon	Sergts.	Corporal	Drmrs.	Privates	Total
Present		1		3	3	1	1	1	9	4	6	42	
Absent	1		1	4	8	3			9	10	6	67	
Hospital				1	3	2							
N.E. since Dec. 24						2			3	3	1	11	
Total	1	1	1	8	14	8	1	1	21	17	13	120	

Chapter III.

1797. On account of the severe losses, Lieut.-Colonel Hugh Lyle Carmichael who was appointed to the command on 16th January, 1797, received a special order from His Royal Highness the Commander-in-Chief early in 1797 to recruit its reduced ranks and to superintend its formation and discipline. He had scarcely adopted measures for this purpose when, on the recommendation of Major-General Hunter, it was ordered to the Island of Granada to assist in quelling the brigand insurgents.

To Granada. June, 1797.

The head-quarters were stationed at Fort Gayare, when an occurrence took place not otherwise of moment than affording the Regiment an opportunity of evincing zeal, and steadiness, during a night attack.

1797. On the night of 19th October, H.M.S. "*Favourite*" stood in and cannonaded the fort. Upon this occasion the convalescents in hospital joined their comrades in the ranks, and finally awaited the approach of what was considered the enemy; at daybreak the mistake was discovered, but his excellency the Governor expressed his satisfaction in the following letter:

" Government House,
Granada. " 20th October, 1797.
" The Governor wishes to express through " Lieut.-Colonel Carmichael his entire satisfaction " with the alacrity, zeal, and spirit shewn by the " troops in this garrison during the alarm of last " night: the Governor thinks he should be wanting " in justice to Lieut.-Colonel Carmichael if he " omitted on this occasion to request that he would " accept his most grateful thanks for the zealous " and officer-like manner he discharged the duties " attached to his situation as senior officer of the " troops in this Government. With a garrison so " composed, the Governor feels a perfect reliance " that no hostile attempt can ever succeed against " this island.
" (Signed) CHARLES GREEN,
" Brigadier-General."

1798. The 2nd West India was the first regiment in the West Indies to propose a voluntary subscription in support of the prosecution of the war, of which the following is an acknowledgment:

Regiment offers to contribute part of their pay towards expenses of the War.

" Government House,
" March 31st, 1798.
" SIR,
" I have been honoured with your letter " expressive of the resolution entered into by the " officers 2nd West India Regiment to request " permission to offer his majesty one month's pay

1798. " towards defraying the expenses of carrying on " this war: also the loyal proposal made by the " non-commissioned officers and privates to be " allowed to contribute two weeks' pay for the " same purpose.

" The sentiments to their sovereign, which
Granada. " their spontaneous offers of assistance so strongly " evinced in his majesty's 2nd West India Regi- " ment, reflects high credit on them.

" (Signed) CHARLES GREEN,
" Brigadier-General."

1799.
The first inspection of the regiment was
1st Inspection made by General Bowyer, the Commander-in-Chief, who issued the following General Orders :

" Head Quarters,
" Granada, 7th January, 1799.

" The Commander-in-Chief has been much " satisfied with the appearance of the 2nd West " India Regiment under arms this morning. His " excellency desires Lieut.-Colonel Carmichael " and the rest of the officers of the corps to accept " his thanks for the zeal and exertion they must " have employed in bringing their men to so for- " ward a state of discipline.

" The General will not fail to report to Field " Marshal His Royal Highness the Duke of York " his favourable opinion of their conduct."

1800.
On the 1st January, 1800, the regiment was
Granada. presented with their first colours by his excellency
1st Colours. Brigadier-General Green. Upon this interesting occasion the regiment, marching under them, took, individually, a solemn obligation to protect them.

During the earlier part of 1800 the Regiment was constantly employed against the Caribs, who still carried on a desultory warfare.

1800. Move to Trinidad.

Jamaica at this period, being not only threatened with invasion, but also a prey to internal commotion, an increase of troops was considered necessary, and in August the 2nd West West India received orders to proceed there. However, while in the act of embarking their baggage, Brigadier-General Green, commanding troops, communicated with Lieutenant-Colonel Carmichael his "having received despatches from "his excellency the Commander-in-Chief, that "the Island of Trinidad was then supposed to be "attacked in force from Guadaloupe; that his "excellency had expressed himself in high terms "of the regiment, leaving it optional with Lieut.-"Colonel Carmichael (as being the senior to "Lieut.-Colonel Picton, Governor of Trinidad) "whether he would take the entire regiment to the "relief of the island, or send a strong detachment "under a field officer." The point of etiquette was immediately waived, and the entire regiment embarked the same day on H.M.S. "*Dromedary*." Light winds and strong currents baffled the first and second attempts to enter the Gulf of Paria;

1800. Loss of H.M.S. "Dromedary."

but on account of the urgency of the service, a third attempt was made at night. However, the wind falling at a critical moment, the ship was swept away by the strong currents which prevail there, and carried with great force on to the Marasol rock: from the force of the breakers, and the abrupt height of the rock, no prospect at first appeared of any lives being saved. The ladies, women, and children, were put into boats, as their only chance of escape.

At daybreak, the sea having moderated, a sailor succeeded in swimming to the rock to which he attached a line, and then the whole of the troops and crew, amounting in all to over 500, with the assistance of spars, &c., succeeded in landing on the rock. One hogshead of water and some

1800. Trinidad. 13th August.

biscuits only could be saved. The ship, breaking up immediately, sunk in deep water; all the stores, baggage, &c., going down with her: nothing was recovered. The boats containing the women and children, contrary to expectation, succeeded in making a landing at Trinidad, and prompt assistance was sent by the governor, Lieut.-Colonel Picton, and the regiment was rescued from their perilous situation, having been thirty (30) hours on the rock, practically without food.

To the good discipline observed on this occasion must be attributed the fact that not a single life was lost; many officers' lives were saved owing to the attachment of their men, who swam with, and supported them through the heavy surf, also, that although all their kits and baggage were lost, the men succeeded in saving nearly all their muskets, only sixty-four (64) out of four hundred (400) stand of arms being missing on their arrival at Trinidad.

The whole of the regimental books and records were lost, and with it the early history of the regiment. This loss was most keenly felt.

13th August, 1800. Garrison Orders. Trinidad.

Upon the arrival of the regiment at Trinidad the following garrison order was published by the Governor:

" Port of Spain, August 13th, 1800.
" The Commandant congratulates Lieut.-
" Colonel Carmichael and the 2nd West India
" Regiment on their miraculous escape, an event
" highly honourable to the Corps, as nothing less
" than the extraordinary good order and patient
" obedience so remarkable in the whole Corps on
"this occasion, could have rendered the event so
" complete."

1800. H.E. Lieut.-General Triggs, the Commander-in-Chief in the Leward Islands, "with his "marked approbation," ordered an immediate grant for the indemnification of all losses sustained.

Trinidad.

Upon the receipt at Granada of the news of the loss of the "*Dromedary*," the general officer commanding—Brigadier-General Green—wrote *a letter to the regiment* conveying "his congratulation "at the happy result of their good order and dis- "cipline." The authorities of that island, at the same time, availed themselves "of this, the earli- "est opportunity of marking their sense of the "benefits derived from the service of the 2nd West "India Regiment, and which its sudden departure "had precluded," by transmitting unanimous resolutions to that effect, of the Council, and the House of Assembly, in separate addresses, through the president, and speaker, to Lieut.-Colonel Carmichael, the officers, and regiment, dated 18th September, 1800.

In November, Lieut. Potter was specially promoted for distinguished conduct and bravery shewn at the time of the loss of the "*Dromedary*."

" November 15th, 1800.

" SIR,

" I am directed by the Commander-in-Chief "to request you will communicate to Lieut.- "Colonel Carmichael, of the 2nd West India "Regiment, that his excellency is happy to have "an opportunity of shewing his approbation of the "conduct of the corps by appointing Lieut. "Potter to the company that now appears to be "vacant by the change of Captain Brown to

1800. "another corps.

" I have the honour to be,

" &c., &c.,

" (Signed) A. GLADSTONES.

" To

" Lieut.-Col. PICTON,

" Commanding Trinidad.

1801.

Expedition against Danish West Indies.

The meditated attack upon Trinidad having been frustrated, the regiment was ordered to join, in March, 1801, the expedition under command of Lieut.-General Triggs, and Rear-Admiral Duckworth, against the Danish and Swedish West Indies.

The cause of hostilities was a confederation, entered into by Sweden, Denmark, and Russia, to support an armed neutrality. The force destined for the purpose consisted of the 3rd and 11th, 2nd W.I. and 8th W.I. Regiments, the whole under command of Lieut.-Gen. Triggs. The expeditionary force appeared before the Swedish colony of St. Bartholomew on the 19th March, and as that island had a garrison of 21 men only, it surrendered at once.

Capture of St. Martin.

The force being reinforced by other troops from England — including 1st Foot— St. Martin was next attacked; this island was in joint occupation of French and Dutch. The fleet stood into Little Cole Bay on the morning of the 24th March, and the troops got ready for embarkation. One brigade—consisting of 1,800 men, composed of 1st, 11th, and 2nd W.I. Regiment— were told off to attack Fort Chesterfield, near the town of Marigol, on the French portion of the island; the 2nd brigade was to land at Fort Ansterdam, to reduce that fort and the town of Philipsburgh on the Dutch portion.

1801.

It was expected that the principal resistance would be made at Fort Chesterfield. It was necessary to take possession of a hill which commanded the fort, and the 2nd West India was directed to do this. The enemy, perceiving the importance of the position, also attempted to occupy it. The regiment, by a rapid movement, gained the height, repulsed the enemy, and the whole brigade, advancing, took possession of the heights, dragging up their artillery, and made immediate preparation for storming the fort. The governor, seeing his position in the fort was now untenable, at once surrendered.

Capture of Dutch West Indies.

The 2nd brigade—after a sharp action, in which the 8th West India behaved with the utmost gallantry—compelled Fort Ansterdam to surrender before the close of the day, and thus completed the conquest of that island.

From St. Martin, the fleet proceeded to St. Thomas, St. John's, and San Crœx, all of which islands surrendered without resistance.

Jamaica.

In April, the regiment was ordered to Jamaica.

1801. Capture of Dutch West Indies.

The following letter from His Royal Highness the Commander-in-Chief was received about this time:

" Horse Guards,

" 10th February, 1801.

" Sir,

" In the absence of Colonel Brownrigg, I
" had the honour to lay before the Commander-in-
" Chief your letter of 18th October last, together
" with a return of the officers of the regiment un-
" der your command, and copies of letters from

1801. "Lieut.-General Triggs, and Brigadier-General "Green, with public documents, all bearing "honourable testimony to the merit and good con-"duct of the officers and soldiers of the 2nd West "India Regiment, on all occasions, and particularly "on the loss of H.M.S. "*Dromedary*," when their "exertions were so fully and zealously displayed.

" I have it in command to reply to you "His Royal Highness's approbation of the con-"duct of the officers and soldiers of the 2nd "West India Regiment in the instances stated, "and the satisfaction it affords His Royal High-"ness to have occasion to have to report his "favourable opinion of that Corps.

" (Signed) R. MATTHEWS.

" Lieut.-Colonel Carmichael,

" 2nd West India Regt."

1801. Jamaica. The arrival of the Regiment at Jamaica awoke a storm of indignation. When the British Government first proposed the raising of black troops, the project was received in every island with marked disfavour. In 1794, the Barbados House of Assembly moved a resolution to the effect that black troops would prove rather means of destruction to the island than its defence. The Assembly of Jamaica was no less determined in their opposition, and refused to make any provision for the 6th W.I. Regiment.

Public meetings were held throughout the island, and so much was the idea dreaded and disliked, that the House of Assembly passed a resolution to the effect that even if negroes were enlisted in Jamaica for service elsewhere, it would be necessary for the House to adopt measures to prevent their return to the island. As a compromise, the British Government offered to send two

1801. Jamaica. European battalions to Jamaica, provided the island furnished the pay; this was agreed to, and the 1st and 4th Battalions of the 60th were sent in 1794, and the difficulty was considered as finally settled by the people of Jamaica; when, suddenly in April, 1801, the 2nd West India was moved to Jamaica. The excitement in the Island tremendous, the British Government was charged with breaking faith.

The House of Assembly urgently prayed the Home Authorities to remove men whom they considered enemies in disguise. As they, however, remained firm, the House of Assembly declared that they were released from their agreement to provide pay for the two European battalions. This policy not being palatable to the Imperial Government, an offer was made on the 17th June, 1802, to the effect that, if the Colony would consent to undertake the maintenance of the entire force stationed in the island, the British Government would withdraw the 2nd West India, but "that "otherwise, the intention of removing the black "troops must be set aside."

1802. Jamaica. The Regiment was actually embarked on 14th June, 1802, on H.M.S. "*Druid*," but the Assembly having rejected the terms of the British Government, the Regiment was again disembarked and resumed their former stations.

The following G.O. was published while the Regiment was on board ship.

" Deputy-Adjutant-General's Office,
" 16th June, 1802.
" G.O.
" The Commander-in-Chief requests the "officers, non-commissioned officers, and privates "of the 2nd West India Regiment to accept his

1802. Jamaica. "thanks for their good conduct during the period "he has had the honour to command them in "Jamaica.

"(Signed) A. GOULD, M. Brigade."

The establishment of the Regiment at this date was 600 rank and file. During this and the next year (1802-3), martial law being enforced, the Regiment was split up into various detachments all over the island.

1804. 2 Companies to Bahamas. Extra troops being required in 1804 for protection of the Bahamas, two (2) picked companies of the Regiment were despatched there on the 15th September, and, at the same time, the establishment of the rank and file of the Regiment was raised from 600 to 1,000.

1804. Jamaica. About this time, Admiral Cochrane's squadron arrived, and, thus removing all apprehension of invasion, martial law was abolished. The various detachments of the Regiment were ordered into head-quarters, and every attention was directed to the discipline and drill of the new recruits.

1805. French Threaten. On the 1st April, 1805, a French squadron, under command of Admiral Meissiessi, consisting of five sail of the line, two brigs, and two schooners, having on board a strong force, under command of General Le Grange, appeared off the island. Martial law was again proclaimed, and the troops held in immediate readiness to repel a landing.

Finding the island too well prepared to offer the chance of a successful attack, this armament sailed for Dominica, where they succeeded in levying £10,000 sterling on the inhabitants, and returned at once to Europe, without effecting any purpose beyond this one act of pillage.

1805. **Jamaica.**

During the following month (May, 1805) the French Fleet, which had made its escape from the blockade of Toulon, arrived in the West Indies. This Fleet, under the command of Admirals Gravina, Villeuneve, and Dumonoir, consisted of seventeen sail of the line, and to oppose them there was no British Fleet sufficiently strong.

The importance of Jamaica, marking it as a most probable point of attack, every means were devised for its defence.

The uncertainty as to the direction from which the attack would come, and the place the enemy would select for disembarkation, made the duties of the troops of a most harassing nature, and as the 2nd West India was able to stand more fatigue and hardship in that climate than European troops, they had consequently more moving about, and hurried marches, than the others. However, Lord Nelson arriving at Barbados on the 3rd June, the French immediately sailed for Europe, pursued by the British Fleet.

1805. **Fort Augusta** **Jamaica.**

Shortly after this, Sir Thomas Duckworth defeated a French fleet under command of Admiral Lesseiques off St. Domingo, which rendered Jamaica quite secure, in consequence of which, the outlying detachments were withdrawn, and the Regiment was concentrated at Fort Augusta.

In general orders of the 27th December, 1805, the Regiment received, with other troops in the island, the thanks of His Royal Highness the Commander-in-Chief for their exemplary conduct.

1807. **Gunners**

In July and August, 1807, the two companies detached to Nassau rejoined the headquarters, and during this year the idea of training a portion of the Regiment as Artillery was first started. The wisdom of this judicious measure was subsequently well proved.

CHAPTER IV.

1808.

Sir B. Durgan to Command.

On 7th January, 1808, Sir B. Durgan succeeded to the command.

Mutiny of Recruits.

In this year, an occurrence took place, although distressing from the loss of two esteemed lives (Major Darley and Lieut. and Adjt. Ellis), yet was so far from being a stain on the military reputation of the Regiment, that it afforded a melancholy, though signal opportunity of proving its loyalty and devoted the attachment of the men to their officers.

The Regiment, nearly 1,000 strong, was stationed at Fort Augusta. Early in May of that year, a number of slaves, natives of Chama and Cormantine, on the Gold Coast, who had been purchased by the Government, to serve in the West India Regiments, were drafted into the 2nd West India as recruits. While 33 of them were at drill, on the 27th May, under the superintendence of a sergeant, and a corporal, they shewed signs of discontent and insubordination, and, at length,

1808. Mutiny of Recruits.

with bayonets fixed, forced their way out of the fort, to the place where the Regiment was being drilled, under the command of Major Darley, who, accompanied by Lieut. and Adjutant Ellis, rode up to ascertain the cause of the disturbance, and were both instantly bayonetted. The barrack guard, which had already killed some of the mutineers inside the fort, was joined by a general rush of the Regiment, enraged by the deaths of their officers, attacked the recruits at once, and, notwithstanding that every effort was made to restrain them by their officers, killed nine (9) mutineers on the spot, one other dying shortly afterwards from the effect of wounds, 17 in all being killed—the others (16) escaped into the bush, but a cordon of the Regiment being drawn round them, they were soon re-taken, tried, and convicted before a general court-martial, six being shot, and ten pardoned, these, by their subsequent good conduct, redeemed their characters. Some of them were, in 1833, highly esteemed respectable non-commissioned officers.

The following is the opinion of the Court of Inquiry assembled on the day of the occurrence.

"That the Court, having examined, by an "interpreter, several men of the Regiment, of the "same African nation, with the mutineers, cannot "find that the mutiny was any more than amongst "the recruits, nor can the Court find any cause for "the inhuman outrage, beyond the violence of the "party at drill in question, but, on the contrary, the "general conduct of the Regiment has been steady "in every respect, and creditable to itself in the "unfortunate affair of this morning: displaying, "by its conduct against the deluded mutineers, its "attachment to their officers, and obedience to "their orders. It appears to the Court that no

1808. Jamaica.

"violence had been used against the recruits, and "at the time they broke out of the fort, they had "been ordered to stand at ease, and the sergeant "had quitted them for some necessary purpose: "the corporal, who attempted to restrain them, "was wounded.

" (Signed) J. SKERRETT,
" M.-General.

"Held at Fort Augusta,
" 27th May, 1808."

Decorations for gallantry in connection with Mutiny of Recruits. Medal and £5.

His Royal Highness the Commander-in-Chief testified to the high opinion he held of the conduct of the Regiment on this occasion by ordering a gratuity of £5 sterling, with a silver medal, to be given to each of the under-mentioned N.C. officers and men, "as a permanent testimo-"nial of their faithful service upon that occasion."

To Sergeant Alexander Houston, for turning out his guard upon the first alarm, and having immediately attacked the mutineers.

To Sergeant Clarke, for his gallantry in interposing his own person and rescuing thereby an officer from a situation of imminent danger.

To Private Peter Tracey, whose prompt assistance was unable to save Major Darley's life, but who attacked and killed his murderer, in which service he received two severe bayonet wounds.

To Privates Sampson Godfrey, and John Patton, who defended their posts as sentinels at the picquet, until overpowered by numbers, both severely wounded.

Major-General Carmichael, commanding the forces in Jamaica, to shew his undiminished confidence, ordered the 2nd West India to furnish the

1808. daily guard at his residence in the neighbourhood of Kingston.

NOTE.—On the beach, between Port Henderson and Fort Augusta, there is still (1895) a tablet erected to the memory of Major Darley, and also one to Major George Crawford, 2nd West India, who died on 25th December, 1807.

1809. St. Domingo. The next service the Regiment was engaged on was to assist the Spanish in driving the French out of St. Domingo.

In 1802, the French had captured the City of St. Domingo from the Spanish, and had brought the whole of the Spanish portion of the island under the French rule, but, in 1808, news was received that Spain had thrown off the French yoke.

The Spanish in the island rose, under Rameriz, to expel the French. They succeeded, in the autumn of 1808, in cooping up the French in the Cities of St. Domingo and Samana, where, however, the latter were able to hold their ground. The besiegers, although assisted by the British Navy, were not strong enough to make them surrender.

In the spring of 1809, it was determined to assist the Spanish with troops, and Major-General Carmichael was ordered to bring from Jamaica all the available troops then in that Island. Accordingly, an expedition, consisting of 1,400 men, embarked, on the 3rd June, for St. Domingo, including the flank companies, and 100 trained Artillerymen of the 2nd West India.

The transports were crowded, and, unfortunately experienced very bad weather: the ship carrying the 2nd West India having to put into Jacmel in distress.

1809.
St. Domingo.
Offers to pay for Transport

The men were so impatient to reach their destination, that, while at Jacmel, they volunteered to subscribe four dollars a-piece to pay for a schooner to carry them on. After a delay, the expedition reached Palinqui, which is about 30 miles distant from St. Domingo, and disembarked on the 28th June. On the next day, the General reconnoitred the fortifications, which he determined to carry by assault. On the evening of the 30th, he established himself, with a detachment of Spanish troops, on St. Carlos, a hill which commanded, and was within musket range, of the town. On the night of the 1st July, the British troops arrived.

They had been delayed by heavy and incessant rain, and swollen rivers, and had suffered the greatest fatigue in dragging the artillery along bad roads.

The French General opened negociations on on the 3rd, but his proposals being inadmissable, the conference was broken off on the 8th, and everything was got ready for an immediate assault. During this delay, the troops suffered great hardships from the inclemency of the weather, and the difficulty of obtaining supplies. It was considered that an assault would cause less loss, than protracted siege operations during the rainy season. Fifty of the 2nd West India, and an equal number Porto Rico Regiment, were ordered to hold the Church of St. Carlos, as long as the walls remained, 20 guns and 1 mortar bearing on it, at a distance of 388 yds., but, on the preparations being completed, the enemy signified their desire to surrender, which they accordingly did; 1,200 French troops laying down their arms, as prisoners of war. The Regiment re-embarked on 22nd August and arrived at Jamaica on the 31st.

1809. St. Domingo. The following reference to the Regiment was made in local general orders on disembarking at Jamaica.

Jamaica. "General Orders. 1st September, 1809.
" No. 2.
" Of this latter Corps, an accident afforded "a trait in their character which merits notice; "having put into Jacmel in distress, and the trans- "port being thereby delayed, the light company "under Captain Ross, volunteered a march of "more than 300 miles over the mountains, to join "the British Forces, then before the enemy; on "being informed that it was impracticable by land, "they proposed subscribing four dollars each to be "stopped out of their pay, to hire a vessel to carry "them more rapidly to join the Army. This "soldier-like feeling in this company was in unison "with the future good conduct of the Corps. "When other regiments had suffered to extremity "from a sudden and fatal sickness, the most "severe and fatiguing duties entirely devolved up- "on this Regiment, which they not only cheerfully "performed, but, as testified in letters to the "officer commanding by the Deputy-Quartermas- "ter-General and the Deputy-Adjutant-General, "they also contributed as orderlies and attendants "on the hospital, to the preservation of many "valuable lives of soldiers."

1809-1816. Bahamas. In December, 1809, the Regiment moved to the Bahamas, in relief of the 7th West India, ordered to Curaçoa.

1814. America. On the 13th December, 1814, the flank companies embarked on board H.M.S. "*Rota*," to join the expedition, under General Ross and Admiral Sir George Cockburn, against the United States of America. The "*Rota*" arrived at the rendezvous, off Cumberland Island, Georgia, and found there a strong naval force: neither the

1814-1815. Georgia. Admiral nor General, with the remainder of the troops, having arrived, Captain Barry, H.M.S. "*Dragon*," deemed it expedient to strike a blow; two battalions of marines and the 2nd West India under command of Colonel Williams, R.M., effected a landing on Cumberland Island without much opposition, the Americans retiring in gunboats under cover of Fort Peitrie at the entrance of the river St. Mary. The troops next morning crossed to the mainland, and supported by the fire from some gunboats proceeded to attack the fort. The column, headed by the 2nd West India, had proceeded but a short distance by a narrow road through a swampy and densely-wooded country, when it was attacked by a strong body of American riflemen, securely posted behind a breastwork of felled trees; they had time to pour but one volley into the column before the breastwork was stormed, and after a sharp struggle, carried. The enemy fled, so closely pursued, that both British and Americans rushed pellmell into the fort along a narrow causeway, raised above the level of the swamp.

1815. Storming of Fort Peitrie.

Two guns had been placed by the enemy so as to command the causeway, but they could not under the circumstances be brought into action. The Americans finding the fort simultaneously attacked by the gunboats, continued their flight to the town of St. Mary's.

The fort secured, the pursuit was resumed till interrupted by a branch of the St. Mary's river, which delayed the troops until, the gunboats having arrived, a crossing was effected. Upon the approach of the British, the Americans evacuated the town of St. Mary's, which was immediately occupied by the British; the enemy continuing their retreat to Savannah. In this affair, the troops were employed without rest or intermission for 22 hours.

1814-15. Georgia. Storming of Fort Peitrie.

The force under General Ross not being available to co-operate with the Navy, as was intended, Sir George Cockburn despatched the "*Brune*" to the Bahamas for a reinforcement of the 2nd West India, and on the 15th February 300 rank and file were embarked, and proceeded to Georgia. In the meantime the garrison of St. Mary's had become so reduced through sickness, that it was considered untenable, when threatened by a large force from Savannah under General Scott, and upon his approach the town was evacuated without opposition from the enemy, the forts having been previously destroyed. This was the state of affairs when the "*Brune*" arrived with reinforcements; all further operations were suspended, and, upon official notification of peace with the United States being received, the Regiment sailed for the Bahamas arriving there 13th March.

The following officers—amongst others—of the Regiment were present during the above operations:—

Captain Bradley, Lieut. John G. Anderson, Lieut. Thos. McPherson.

1815. Nassau, Bahamas.

Sir George Cockburn, in communicating with H.E. Governor Cameron, with regard to the service performed by the Regiment, stated "It is "an act of justice to the companies which have "served with me here, under the command of "Captain Bradley, to assure Your Excellency "of the great assistance I have invariably received "from them, and their exemplary and gallant "conduct on every occasion.

" I have, &c.,

" (Signed) GEORGE COCKBURN,

" Rear-Admiral."

1815. Nassau. The following extract from a letter, addressed by Lieut.-Colonel Ross, commanding 2nd West India, to the Deputy-Adjutant-General, Jamaica, dated 18th March, 1815, "I feel much "gratification in forwarding to H.E. the Com-"mander-in-Chief, an extract from a letter I have "been honoured with, from Rear-Admiral "Cockburn, and am truly happy to find that the "men already sent are so highly estimated by him. "The extract is as follows—

" 'In consequence of the distinguished and "'gallant conduct of the two flank companies of "'your Regiment, during a skirmish with the "'enemy, which took place on the advance to St. "'Mary's, I am induced to send the "*Brune*" to "'Nassau, to request His Excellency Governor "'Cameron will permit such further numbers of "'the Regiment under your command to come to "'me, as may be deemed prudent to spare from "'Nassau.'"

1816. New Colours. New colours were presented to the Regiment in 1816, while under the command of Lieut.-Colonel Ross.

1816. Jamaica. The Regiment proceeded to Jamaica, embarking at Nassau on the 16th July, 1816.

1818. Detachment to Belize. In 1818, five (5) companies were ordered from Jamaica for detachment duty at Belize.

1819. Headquarters to Africa. In 1819, head-quarters and five (5) companies were ordered to West Africa, under the following circumstance.

1812-1815. Recruiting Establishment. Bunce Island. In 1812, a recruiting establishment for West India Regiments was formed at Bunce Island, Sierra Leone, and an officer of each West India Regiment was stationed there. Ensign Campbell was detailed for this duty. In 1815 there were 700 recruits then under training. Ensign Campbell died there in June, 1815.

1818. On the transfer of Senegal and Goree to the French in 1818, six companies of the Royal African Corps proceeded to the Cape of Good Hope, to be amalgamated with other corps. The three remaining companies were ordered to be disbanded at Sierra Leone, and it was decided to garrison the West Coast with West India troops, and head-quarters and five (5) companies, under command of Lieut.-Colonel Ross, embarked in transports, "*John*" and "*Alfred*," on the 23rd March, 1819, arriving at Sierra Leone on 23rd and 24th May.

The following officers accompanied the head-quarters to Africa :—

Lieut.-Colonel Ross, commanding, Major McPherson ; Capts. Hance, Fitzgerald, and Ricketts; Lieuts. Hales, Heald, McLean, and Stepney; Ensigns Lowe, Dawson, and Moriarty, and 341 N.C. officers and men, distributed as follows :—

Sierra Leone - 194;
Gambia - - - 106;
Isles de Los - - 34;
Banana Island - - 7.

1819. The remaining five (5) companies left in the West Indies were stationed—three companies at Honduras, two companies at Bahamas.

Before leaving Jamaica, Major-General Conran, commanding the Forces, issued the following General Order.

G.O. Jamaica. "To express his high approbation of its " services in this command, the good conduct and " fidelity it has maintained here, has impressed " him with the most favourable opinion of its value " in the West Indies.

1819. West Africa.

"The regularity and attention of the Regi- "ment in its military duties, and the orderly and "civil deportment of the men to the community at "large, in this wealthy and populous city (King- "ston) have been universally acknowledged."

The detachment at Isles de Los was stationed at Crawford Island. At this time the 2nd West India were the only troops in West Africa. Sir Charles McCarthy in a letter dated June, 1819, says "The five companies 2nd West "Indian Regiment are now the only corps serving "on the Coast, and as he considers that force in- "adequate even in time of peace for the defence "of the Colonial possessions he suggests that the "remainder of the Regiment, or one or two com- "panies of European soldiers should be sent out so "as to arrive in November or December."

In July, 1819, the middle of the rainy season, the barracks at Isles de Los were burned down and the detachment remained without any proper shelter till the following December. The three officers stationed there were sick the whole time, the European sergeant and his wife died. The three officers are described by the principal medical officer in his return as living "in one room in a native hut which is not weather tight."

Severe loss from climate.

Before the wing of the Regiment had been eight months on the Coast, three out of the twelve officers who had come across with it from the West Indies had died as follows :—

Ensign Lowe at Gambia on the 12th August, 1819, Lieut. Heald at Isle de Los on the 2nd January, 1820, and Lieut. Hales at Sierra Leone, on the 13th January, 1820; in addition to the above, in August, 1819, the wife of Major McPherson, two children of Captain Fitzgerald,

1819. and one child of Lieut. Hales all died, while in January, 1820 another child of Captain Fitzgerald died.

1820. Rio Pongo Expedition.

In May, 1820, a midshipman named Robert Inman, of H.M.S. brig "*Thistle*," commanded by Lieut. Commander Hagen was murdered with several of his boat's crew, up the Rio Pongo, near Sierra Leone, whither he had been sent to capture a slave vessel.

The authors of this crime were natives acting under the orders of a European slave dealer named Curtis, who had large barracoons on the river; and to punish this outrage three companies of the regiment, under command of Captain James Chisholm, embarked on the 10th of May on board H.M.S. "*Myrmidon*" and "*Morgiana*" and H.M. brigs "*Snapper*" and "*Thistle*," sailing from Freetown on the morning of the 12th, and arriving off the mouth of the Rio Pongo on the 15th May. Acting in conjunction with a naval force under command of Captain Lectrie, H.M.S. "*Tartar*." Captain Chisholm reports in his despatch, as follows:—

Capt. Chisholm Despatch.

"As there was not sufficient depth of water "to float the ships on the bar, their boats with the "marines and troops on board were removed to "the brigs, and those vessels continued approaching "the bar, until the lateness of the evening rendered "it necessary to come to an anchor. We reached "the river on the following morning, and on our "arrival at the Forks, a canoe was despatched "with a letter to the native chiefs and traders de- "claratory of our wish to treat with them for the "release of the surviving crew of the boat of H.M. "brig '*Thistle*,' and the restoration of the boat. "We received information that Curtis had received "considerable aid in men and arms from the

1820.
Capt. Chisholm Despatch.

"neighbouring chiefs, and was prepared to offer "an obstinate resistance to our landing; in con- "sequence the brigs were brought as near to his "town as possible, and most of the boats armed "with canonades, to cover the landing of the "troops.

Capture of Curtistown.

" Supposing that the appearance of so con- "siderable a force, as now approached Curtistown, "would induce the natives to enter into negociations "for the release of the seamen in their custody and "the surrender of Curtistown, the boats advanced "under a flag of truce, and from their having (on "our hoisting a truce) exhibited a white flag from "their fort, a mud fortification mounting several "guns, we had reason to believe that they com- "prehended its signification.

" The signal, and our forbearance were "however, totally disregarded, for immediately on "the arrival of the boats at the landing place, a "heavy fire commenced from the fort, and from "parties of men posted in very thick mangrove "close to the wharf: this was instantly returned "on our side; and the whole of the men being "landed, the enemy were compelled to retire to a "palisade erected in front of the town.

" From behind this covering they continued "to oppose our advance, but were soon dislodged, "and being closely pursued retreated through the "town to a wood in its rear.

" Having taken possession of the town and "fort and waited some time in expectation that "some of the natives would attempt to save their "property from destruction, by making advances "towards an accommodation, Captain Leeke of "H.M.S. '*Myrmidon*' (who landed immediately on "the fort being silenced by the fire of the most

May, 1820. **Capt. Chisholm Despatch.** **Rio Pongo Expedition.**

"advanced brig) and myself determined upon "destroying the stockades and palisades sur-"rounding the town, burning the houses, rasing "the fort, and removing the cannon from it to the "vessels of war; and on this being done it was "agreed that the troops should proceed to the "attack of the adjoining towns in alliance with "Curtis. During the execution of this service, I "made frequent attempts to invite the natives to a "conference, but my endeavours proving fruitless, "their towns were burnt and the troops returned "to the ships.

" The gentleman (Mr. Wilson) to whom we "had entrusted the letter addressed to the chiefs "and traders on the 16th, came on H.M. brig "'*Snapper*" soon after our re-embarkation, and it "appearing by his statement that Mungo Brama, "a chief of considerable power, residing about "four miles from Curtistown, was the principal "encourager of the attack on the '*Thistle's*' boat, "and the person at whose command the wounded "prisoners were inhumanly treated after their "surrender. Captain Leeke and myself thought "it probable that the few surviving seamen might "be still in his town, and it was therefore de-"termined that the troops should visit it early in "the morning with the view of demanding their "release; and in the event of their acting hostilely "towards us, it was decided that they should be "considered confederates of Curtis, and their "persons and property dealt with accordingly.

" The town is situated in the middle of an "extensive wood, and as we were exposed during "one march to a very heavy fall of rain, and being "without guides, we found much difficulty in dis-"covering it. We saw but few of the inhabitants, "but from their being armed, and having attempted "resistance I have great reason to believe that

1820. Capt. Chisholm Despatch. Rio Pongo Expedition.

"they depended upon co-operation of a concealed "body of men much more numerous and powerful "than themselves.

"They suffered considerably from our fire, "and a large quantity of merchandize (principally "the property of Curtis) was destroyed. In the "course of the operations of this and the pre- "ceding day a corporal of marines died from "excessive fatigue, and one private of marines and "two privates of the 2nd West India Regiment "were wounded.

"Shortly after returning to the ships we had "the satisfaction of obtaining the release of two of "the seamen of the "*Thistle*," through King "Yanda Coney, who becoming anxious for the "safety of his town, insisted on their liberation. "The four remaining seamen were secured from "the power of Curtis, through the good offices of "Mr. Wilson, and we had the pleasure of receiving "them on board.

"The principal object of the expedition "being accomplished by the restoration of these "men to the service of their country and the "punishment of the savages, who so barbarously "put their comrades to death, the squadron "returned to Sierra Leone, arriving there on "May 24th.

"I feel great pleasure in reporting to you "that the behaviour of the troops has been highly "satisfactory. The conquest of a large district of "wooded country, defended by an armed body of "men, which the neighbouring inhabitants say ex- "ceeded three thousand five hundred, and the des- "truction of seven towns, with an inconsiderable loss "on our side, is to be ascribed to the resolute "conduct of the conjoined forces in the attack on "Curtistown."

Chapter V.

1823. Ashanti War. In March, 1823, the British Government took over all the Forts on the Gold Coast in possession of the African Company, and the native troops in pay of the Company were formed into a Colonial corps and named the "Royal African Colonial Corps of Light Infantry," consisting of three companies. Captain Chisholm and Lieut. Laing were transferred to it from the 2nd West India, with the rank of Major and Captain respectively.

The Governor Sir Charles McCarthy found on assuming the Government of the Forts that the Ashantis had been giving trouble, and that all trade between Cape Coast and Ashanti had ceased.

In November, 1822, a sergeant, R.A. Colonial Corps was kidnapped by the Ashantis at Anamaloo, taken to Dunquah, some 20 miles inland, where he was kept prisoner till 1st February, 1823, when he was put to death. Sir Charles McCarthy, who had returned from Sierra Leone in December, 1822, bringing with him one company, 2nd West India, determined to punish this outrage, and on the evening of 21st February, an expeditionary force composed of the company, 2nd West India and the Royal African Colonial Corps, and some natives started for Dunquah.

1823. Action at Dunquah.

" From treachery, however, or imbecility of "the Guides, the troops which ought to have "reached Dunquah at 4 o'clock in the morning, lost "the right road, and after excessive fatigue and "want of every sort of provisions were suddenly "attacked under a heavy fire by a numerous force "of Ashantis and Fantees, ambushed in a thick "covered wood, on both sides of a very narrow "rugged path; but the advanced guard, consisting "of a few men of the 2nd West Indian Regiment, "under command of Captain Laing, Royal African "Corps and Ensign Wetherell, 2nd West Indian "Regiment, returned the fire and moved onward. "But finding that they had been led into a different "direction from Dunquah, it was conceived ad-"visable that the expedition should fall back on "Anamaloo. In this affair there were six men "killed, one officer, Lieut. Swanzy, Royal African "Corps, and 38 men wounded and four missing." (*Ricketts*).

1823. Ashanti War

Shortly after the 17th May, Sir Charles McCarthy left for Sierra Leone, leaving Major Chisholm in command. On the 4th June, 3,000 Ashantis crossed the Prah, having sent word beforehand to the effect that they were coming down to drive the English into the sea. Captain Laing, with all the available troops, and a large contingent of natives, was despatched to meet them. On hearing of this the Ashantis at once retired across the Prah. The troops returned having first destroyed the chief of Essecumah's town as he had refused to assist the British.

On the 28th July, the Ashantis again advanced across the Prah and Captain Laing moved his force to Yan Coomassie-Fanti, and from there by forced marches to Essecumah, which he found the Ashantis had that very morning occupied after a sharp skirmish with some loyal Fantees.

1823. Ashanti War. "The appearance of the troops caused the "enemy to abandon the place in great disorder, "and without any resistance; they with their "accustomed cruelty massacred the unfortunate "prisoners who had fallen into their hands, whose "bodies were found still reeking from the bruises "of their murderers. The near approach of night "prevented the troops from pursuing them, and "having halted till morning they marched to the "westward in search of the enemy, in which "direction it was conceived they would fall in with "them. The attack was planned in five divisions "and they came upon the camp unobserved, "which was immediately deserted by the enemy, "leaving their dinners on the fire." (*Ricketts*).

The troops now returned to Cape Coast; outposts at Mansu, 50 miles north, and at Jooquah 18 miles nor-west were formed of natives and local troops.

Sir Charles McCarthy returned from Sierra Leone on the 28th November. In the meantime at his request, the Europeans of the Royal African Corps who, on the disbandment of that corps, had been sent to the Cape of Good Hope, were recalled so now there was a company of Europeans at Cape Coast.

Towards the end of December, news reached the Coast that the Ashantis had again crossed the Prah, and were advancing rapidly on Cape Coast.

1824. The company 2nd West India and Royal African Corps were sent to Jooquah on the 27th, and on the 28th the militia joined them, the native levies coming in quickly, so that by the 4th January, 1824, a force of 2,000 had been collected. On the 8th the main body moved to Ampenasu, a village on the Prah, about 18 miles north of Jooquah, Major Chisholm in command.

1824. On the 8th January, Sir C. McCarthy, having received information that the Ashantis had entered the Wassaw country, marched on the 9th with a Fantee company, Royal African Colonial Corps, 80 strong, three companies native militia (170) and about 240 unorganized natives, leaving all the regulars at Jooquah. He was accompanied by Capt. Ricketts and Ensign Wetherell 2nd West India, the former as Brigade Major, the latter as private secretary, also Surgeon Tedley and two privates 2nd West India as orderlies: reached Assamacow on the 14th. On the 17th, orders were sent to Major Chisholm to bring up his force, but unfortunately the messenger being unacquainted with the country did not reach Major Chisholm until the 22nd. He on receipt of the order marched at once, but too late; for on the 21st the Ashantis attacked Assamacow, killing Sir Charles McCarthy and all his staff, except Captain Ricketts, who escaped and reached Major Chisholm on the 24th.

Battle of Assamacow. Defeat and Death of Sir C. McCarthy.

Major Chisholm not considering his force strong enough to cope with the victorious enemy, at once commanded a retreat to the Coast, reaching Cape Coast on the evening of the 27th January.

The following is the return of killed and wounded in this most unfortunate affair.

Killed and missing Officers.

Brigadier General Sir C. McCarthy, commanding; Ensign Wetherell and Surgeon Tedley, 2nd West India Regiment; Captains Heddle, Jones and Raydon, Royal Cape Coast Militia; Mr. S. Buckle, Col. Engineer and Col. A.D.C. to His Excellency Sir C. McCarthy; Captain Robertson, Royal Volunteer Company; Mr. Brandon, Acting Ordnance Store Keeper.

1824.
Ashanti War.

Killed and missing Men.

1 private, 2nd W.I.R.		
41 N.C.O's and men,		R.A.C. Corps.
81 ,,	,,	R.C.C. Militia.
54 ,,	,,	Royal Volunteers.

Wounded.

Captain Ricketts, 2nd	W.I. Regiment.
Ensign Erskine	R.A.C. Corps.
One private	2nd W.I. Regiment.
17 N.C.O's and men	R.A.C. Corps
58 ,, ,,	R.C.C. Militia.
14 ,, ,,	R. Volunteers.

"It appeared by Mr. Williams' statement "that he left the field of action in company with "Sir C. McCarthy, Mr. Buckle and Ensign "Wetherell, and after proceeding a short distance "along the track to Assamacow, they were suddenly "attacked by a party of the enemy, who fired and "broke one of Sir C. McCarthy's arms, and that "he immediately after received another wound in "the chest and fell. They removed him under a "tree, where all remained waiting their fate, "which they perceived to be inevitable. Im-"mediately afterwards Mr. Williams received a "ball in his thigh, which rendered him senseless; "previous however to his falling, he saw Ensign "Wetherell who appeared also to have been "wounded, lying close to Sir Charles, cutting with "his sword at the enemy, as they were tearing the "clothes off his friend and patron. Mr. Williams "upon recovering his senses perceived that some "Ashantis were attempting to cut off his head, "and had already inflicted one gash on the back "of his neck. Luckily, however, at this crisis, an "Ashanti of authority came up and recognizing "Mr. Williams, from whom he had received some "kindness in the African Company's time, with-

1824. Ashanti War.

"held the hand of the savage. On Mr. Williams "recovering his senses, he saw the headless trunk "of Sir Charles McCarthy, Mr. Buckle and "Ensign Wetherell." (*Ricketts.*)

The defeat of Sir C. McCarthy had a very dispiriting effect upon the native chiefs, and there was considerable difficulty in persuading them to continue their co-operation. On the 5th February, a camp was again formed at Jooquah, and on the 14th the force marched to Commendah, and left that place on the 16th in H.M.S. "*Bann*" and "*Owen Glendower*" for Dutch Secondee; this place they destroyed as a punishment on the natives for acts of hostility against the fugitives from the Battle of Assamacow, and at once returned to Commendah. Towards the end of February news came in that the Ashantis were preparing to advance again across the Prah. Captain Ricketts, 2nd West India, was ordered to oppose the crossing. Consequently he moved his detachment on the 1st March to Deraboassie, a village on the Prah in the direct route between Assamacow and Commendah, placing Lieut. MacCarthy in command, posted some native allies along the river, and moved with the remainder of his force to the mouth of the Prah, where he encamped.

From the 10th to 31st March, there were constant small skirmishes between the British and the Ashantis, on which latter date a large number of native allies, who had been employed in cutting paths towards the enemy's camp, suddenly became panic stricken, and ran away across the Prah, leaving 2,000 stand of arms, and nearly all the ammunition to be looted by the enemy. Captain Blencama R.A.C. Corps, who had relieved Captain Ricketts on the 10th, finding himself deserted by all of the allies, retired his force to Cape Coast.

1824. Ashanti War. On the 10th April, a camp was formed at Effectee, throwing out an outpost of allies about 12 miles in front. On the 25th April the Ashantis attacked the outpost, the allies flying in all directions, and advanced rapidly on Effectee, this place they took possession of, the British force falling back on Cape Coast. A few days after which the British force advanced to Beulah, about five miles from Cape Coast, and the same distance from Effectee; with great difficulty a large force of natives was collected, and were set to work to cut paths towards the enemy's position. On the 18th May, Lieut.-Col. Sutherland, 2nd West India, arrived with 40 men, and assumed command of the troops, Major Chisholm being left in command at Beulah.

Battle of Beulah. On the 21st an attack was made on Effectee; the action lasted five hours; the enemy fought bravely, keeping up a heavy fire from the bush which was so thick that they could only be seen at intervals. They made several attempts to turn Major Chisholm's flanks; but not being able to drive the British off, at length retreated into the village of Effectee.

At the very beginning of the fight, the Fanti contingent (3,000) fled without firing a shot, and meeting carriers bringing up ammunition and supplies from Cape Coast, reported that the British had been defeated.

They all turned back and made for Cape Coast as fast as they could. In consequence of their cowardice, the troops found themselves at nightfall without ammunition, food or water, and had therefore to fall back on Sweet River, instead of holding their ground gained after such hard fighting.

1824. Ashanti War. The allies who evidently had enough of fighting, dispersed during the night, they having lost 84 killed and 603 wounded out of 5,887.

The following troops, &c. were engaged:—2nd W.I., 2 officers, 99 N.C.O's and men; R.A.C. Corps, 5 officers, 134 N.C.O's and men; of these 9 N.C.O's and men were killed and 20 wounded. Major Chisholm reported that the detachment 2nd West India conducted themselves with very praiseworthy steadiness in this engagement.

The troops now returned to Cape Coast leaving a party of observation at Beulah.

Defence of Cape Coast. Two days after this the Ashantis re-occupied their camp at Effectee, and on the 28th May were reinforced by an army said to be 10,000 strong from Coomassie, commanded by the King, who at once sent a message to Colonel Sutherland that "the walls of the Castle were not "high enough and should be made higher, and "that he ought to land all the guns from the war "ships, as he (the King) intended to throw every "stone of the Castle into the sea."

On the 21st June the enemy advanced to within five miles of Cape Coast, driving in the party from Beulah; and "on the 22nd moved "considerably nearer to Cape Coast, and took up "a position of about three miles in extent: the "bush was so thick, that their strength could only "be judged by the number of their fires. On the "23rd they advanced so near that they were distinctly seen in great force on the heights. An "attack on Cape Coast was consequently momentarily expected, and the male inhabitants of the "town were ordered to muster all possible resistance. The women and children amounting "to nearly five thousand, most of whom had been

1824. Ashanti War.

"driven in from their respective towns and "villages as the enemy had advanced, now rushed "into the Castle, and as only the wicket of the "gate was left open, which admitted only one "person at a time, the screaming of the children, "the melancholy cries of the women squeezing "for entrance was beyond anything which can be "conceived. The seamen and marines from H.M.S. "'*Victor*' and the merchant vessels in the roads "were landed to man the guns and every possible "means were taken for defence." (*Ricketts.*)

The confusion was now increased by a fire which soon involved the town in a general conflagration. On the report of the enemy's advance on the 22nd, Lieut.-Col. Sutherland had ordered some houses, which were close to and overlooked the walls of the Castle, to be pulled down: but the order was not carried out by the town's people, and the garrison was too weak to do it; on the 23rd when the enemy's advance was signalled from Smith's town (now called Fort Victoria), he ordered these houses to be set on fire, and the wind suddenly changing, the fire spread all over the town. The enemy advanced to within one mile of the Castle, but retired next day—24th to Beulah, where they remained till the end of the month, employing their time in laying waste the surrounding country and villages.

At this time the garrison consisted of 360 all ranks, of whom 104 were in Hospital.

On the 4th July, H.M.S. "*Thetis*" arrived from England with a detachment of Europeans for the R.A. Colonial Corps, and Captain Winter and two subalterns, 2nd West India.

On the 6th a force of 5,000 natives arrived from Accra.

1824. Ashanti War.

"On the 7th the Ashantis again occupied "the heights near Cape Coast; the King could be "plainly seen through a glass, he having a large "clearing made round his tent; some of his men "wore the uniforms of our officers, who had been "killed at Assamacow. They also displayed the "English, Dutch and Danish flags with others of "their own making: we were at this moment very "badly supplied with ball, and were obliged to "take all the water pipes from the Castle, the "lead from the tops of the merchants' houses, and "all the pewter pots and pans that could be "procured, the ships furnishing all the lead they "were able to spare, for the purpose of cutting up "into slugs by the sailors, who were kept employed "at this work for many days and nights, both on "board and on shore."—(*Ricketts*). On the 8th, the garrison took up a position on a chain of hills opposite the enemy, and at once employed the native contingent in cutting roads through the bush towards the enemy's position; the troops were employed in reconnoitring the enemy. On the 11th the enemy descended from their position and formed up in the valley in front of the British position, about 800 yards from the town. At about 2 p.m. the engagement commenced and continued till dark, when the enemy retired. The following force was engaged in this action:—Royal Marines, 1 officer, 2 men; 2nd W.I. Regiment, 1 officer, 90 men; Royal A. Col. Corps, 15 officers, 193 men. Total 17 officers, 285 men beside 4,770 local.

The total casualties on the British side were 1 officer and 103 men killed, and 448 men wounded, of which the 2nd West India lost 3 men wounded. On the 12th the Ashantis again made a forward movement but did not attack.

1824. Ashanti War. "On the morning of the 13th they were "again observed in motion, descending in Indian "file through several paths towards the valley from "the height on which the King had pitched his "marquee. A renewal of the engagement was "now hourly expected by us, and we were "accordingly prepared. They still continued "marching down the hills till dark, when numerous "fires were observed in the valleys, but when "daylight appeared not one of them could be "seen." (*Ricketts.*)

Under cover of this manœuvre the whole Ashanti army had retreated, having lost thousands of their men from smallpox, dysentery, and want of food. As the garrison was too weak to pursue, they were allowed to retire unmolested, and they encamped near Beulah, about six miles from the town.

On the 19th July, they commenced their retreat, and thus ended the Ashanti invasion of 1824. This was followed by a time of great hardship and suffering on the part of the garrison. Provisions were very scanty, there being neither meal nor flour; the mortality amongst the Europeans in the garrison was very high from 5 to 6 dying daily including many officers, while the streets of the town were filled with dead and dying: the result of famine and smallpox.

1825. In March, 1825, Major General Turner arrived with 700 soldiers for the Royal African Colonial Corps and 200 of the 2nd West India from Sierra Leone, but finding matters had quieted down decided that the 2nd West India were no longer required, and consequently on the 14th April they sailed for the West Indies direct.

Regiment moved to West Indies.

When they embarked at Sierra Leone on 25th February for the Gold Coast, it was expected,

1825. that they would return to Sierra Leone, prior to going over to the West Indies; consequently their heavy baggage was not embarked, including regimental books and records not required on active service; but as they did not do so, en route for the West Indies, the baggage and books, &c. were left behind, the latter have never since been recovered.

Loss of books and records.

They arrived at Nassau, Bahamas on the 11th July, 1825. The Head Quarters and five companies at Nassau furnishing detachments to Jamaica, Turks Island, and Honduras, one company being left at Sierra Leone for recruiting purposes. On the 30th May, 1827, the regiment was inspected by H. E. the Governor of Bahamas, who published the following Order:

1827. Nassau.

" District Orders, Nassau,
" 30th May, 1827.

" The Governor having inspected the 5 " companies of the 2nd West India Regiment " stationed in the Bahamas has been much pleased " with their appearance on parade, and the steady " and soldier-like manner in which they executed " the manœuvres and firings; everything con- " nected with the regiment which has yet come " under the Governor's observation bears the " mark of zeal and attention on the part of Major " Nicholls and testifies to the creditable support " he has obtained from the officers under his " command.

" It is not alone the public exhibition of " the regiment as a body which the Governor has " to commend: the care and pains of the officer " commanding and those under him are manifested " by the soldierly deportment and appearance of " the men, on occasions when they are not aware " that any notice is taken, or remarks made on

1827. "their proceedings; the Governor will not fail to "report favourably of the regiment to the Com-"mander-in-Chief of the forces, with a view of its "reaching His Grace, the Commander-in-Chief.

" By command,

" (Signed) H. P. WILLIAMS,

" Act. Fort Adj."

1826.
The company at Sierra Leone.

In the meantime the company left at Sierra Leone was seeing some service. In January, 1826, Major General Turner, Governor of Sierra Leone, decided to attack some slave traders at Sherbro, and on the 7th February, he started from Sierra Leone with 50 of the Royal African Colonial Corps and 40 of the 2nd West India. He first attacked the stockades of Rohn, a strong work held by trained men in the service of the slave traders, this they took without much trouble, together with ten pieces of ordnance, one hundred stand of arms, and a quantity of powder and ammunition. He afterwards attacked the town of Macaaba, which was about 15 miles higher up the river, and 8 other strongholds and smaller towns, where hundreds of slaves were found in chains awaiting shipment.

Sherbro Expedition.

The expedition returned to the ships and sailed for Sierra Leone on the 23rd February.

Mortality on the Coast.

The year 1826 was a fatal one for Europeans. Shortly after his return from Sherbro, Major General Turner died of fever. At the Gambia in a few months 210 soldiers died of a total of 250, and at Sierra Leone between the 25th July and 24th August, 60 Europeans Royal A.C. Corps died out of 120—General Campbell's despatch No. 61 of November 29th, 1826—out of 12 artillery men who arrived at Cape Coast with General Turner at the end of March, 1825, only 3 survived to embark for England in July of that year.

1826. In a letter from Governor Macaulay to Lord Bathurst, dated June 28th, 1826, mention is made of a Sergeant, 2nd West India, named Buckhardt, who with 12 men was in sole charge of the Fort and settlement at MacCarthy's Island, he says "the state of the place reflects the greatest "credit on the black sergeant."

1828. Nassau. On the 25th July, 1828, the regiment was again inspected by the Governor of Bahamas, who issued the following order:

" District Orders, Nassau,
" 25th July, 1828.
" His Excellency the Governor having in-"spected the 2nd West India Regiment, feels "it due to Lieut.-Col. MacDonald and the officers, "non-commissioned officers and privates to ex-"press his approbation of the appearance of the "regiment in the field, and their manœuvrings and "firings, and likewise of the respectable and "creditable deportment of the corps in general. "He will not fail to make a favourable report "accordingly.

" By command,
" (Signed) H. P. WILLIAMS,
" Fort Adjutant."

CHAPTER VI.

1830. New Colours 3rd Set.

On the 17th March, 1830, new Colours, the gift of the Colonel, Lieut.-General Sir John Byng, were presented to the Regiment while under the temporary command of Major Nicholls, by Lady Carmichael Smyth. The following account of the proceeding is taken from the Royal Gazette, Demerara, dated 21st August, 1830, presumably contributed by a correspondent at Nassau.

"Presentation of Colours, Nassau, N.P., March, 17th, 1830.

" It was with much satisfaction that we "witnessed this day, the ceremony of presenting a "pair of new Colours to that corps, which we must "call our old and favourite regiment, His "Majesty's 2nd West India, for a part of it and "occasionally the whole of it has been stationed "here for nearly thirty years.

" The regiment being formed in open order "under command of Major Nicholls, the com- "mandant of the garrison, H.E. the Governor and "Lady Carmichael Smyth, with the Lord Bishop,

1831. New Colours. "attended by His Excellency's staff, &c., came on "the ground about 12 o'clock, and proceeded to a "tent erected on the west side of the square, when "the regiment with closed ranks formed three "sides of a square; the Colours having been "placed on a large drum inside the tent, were "then blessed in the usual form by the Rev. M. "Strachan, after which the Grenadiers wheeled to "the right, so as to bring the centre of the com- "pany opposite to where Lady Carmichael Smyth "was sitting, and taking open order, two ensigns "placed themselves in front in a line with the "Grenadier officers; Sir James then took the "King's and immediately afterwards the Regi- "mental Colours, and handed them to Lady "Carmichael Smyth, near whom stood Major "Nicholls, who on receiving them from her "Ladyship, placed them in the hands of the "ensigns, and her Ladyship addressed the regiment "nearly in the following words:—Major Nicholls, "I cannot but feel highly flattered at the honour "you have done me in requesting me to present "the new Colours to the regiment under your "command. I have accepted this office with the "greatest pleasure, because I am confident from "the acquaintance I have had the happiness to "make with the officers of the 2nd West India "Regiment, since my arrival in this colony, that "these Colours will be displayed with zeal and "alacrity, whenever and where ever the services "of their king and country may require them."

To which Major Nicholls replied:—"For "the honour your Ladyship has condescended to "confer upon this regiment on the present in- "teresting occasion, permit me for myself and on "behalf of my brother officers, respectfully to offer "your Ladyship our cordial thanks.

" Could the favour which we have just now

1830. New Colours. "received at your Ladyship's hands be possibly "further enhanced in our grateful estimation, it "would be from the truly delicate, though highly "flattering language with which your Ladyship "has so kindly and so handsomely accompanied "the presentation of our new Colours.

"We also feel deeply complimented by the "confidence expressed by your Ladyship in the "zeal and alacrity, the display of which your "Ladyship has been pleased to anticipate on our "part, under these banners when occasion calls, "in the service of our king and country; a duty, "our devotion to which we beg your Ladyship "to be assured, will never fail to receive, if possible, "additional incitement from the recollection of "this day of which the regiment has such just "reason to be proud."

"The line was then reformed in open order, "and the Grenadiers moved in file through the "ranks to their original position, on arriving at "the left flank the regiment presented arms, and "the new Colours, on reaching the centre of the line "were placed between the two old Colours; the "regiment then shouldered arms; the adjutant "being between the two old Colours, advanced "with them to the front, where the quarter-master "and his sergeant were in waiting with the "apparatus for burning them, and the former "saluting in a most respectful manner received "the king's and then the regimental Colour: the "staves were cut into proper lengths: the precious "remains of the old flags placed over them and "the whole set fire to and burnt.

"The ensigns then faced about, and with "the adjutant returned to the centre, when the "junior gave up the Colours to the two senior "ensigns. The regiment fired three volleys, after

1830. " which the quarter-master collected and deposited " the ashes of the old Colours in a silver vase " made for the purpose. The regiment then " closed ranks and marched past, lodged the " Colours and were dismissed, the officers joined " the party in the tent, where refreshments had " been prepared.

The following District General Order was published:

Nassau. " District General Orders,
" Nassau 17th, March, 1830.
" No. 1.
" Major General Sir James Carmichael " Smyth wishes to repeat in orders, what he had " the pleasure of saying on parade this morning " to the 2nd West India Regiment: namely the " great satisfaction he experienced in witnessing " the clean, steady and soldier-like appearance of " the men under arms. The high state of discipline " of the 2nd West India Regiment shews what " can be made of the African soldiers under good " officers.

" No. 2.
" The Major-General hopes that the regi- " ment will long guard the new Colours this day " confided to their care.

" He begs to assure the officers, non- " commissioned officers and men that there are " very few regiments indeed on whose exertions he " would feel more disposed to place confidence, " should he ever have the good fortune to command " them on service."
" By Command,
" (Signed) J. C. DICKINSON,
" Acting Fort Adjutant.

1830. In December, 1830, the Head-Quarters and Grenadier Company were ordered to Honduras, leaving four companies in the Bahamas.

1831. Capture of Fort Bullen.

In 1831 the recruiting company at Sierra Leone under command of Lieut. Lardner was employed at the Gambia. The following is an extract from Ellis' History 1st West India Regiment:— "In August, 1831, disturbances "having occurred amongst the Mandingoes living "in the neighbourhood of Fort Bullen, Barra Point, "Ensign Fearon of the Royal African Corps by "direction of Lieut.-Governor Rendall, had pro-"ceeded with thirty men of his corps and a few "pensioners on the night of August 22nd to the "stockaded town of Essaw (? Epoue) of Yahassu, "the capital of Barra to demand hostages from "the king. At Essaw, this small force was "attacked by a large body of Mandingoes, and "compelled to retire to Fort Bullen, to which "place the victorious Mandingoes advanced, com-"pletely investing it on the land side. The day "following, Ensign Fearon having lost twenty-"three men out of his little force, evacuated the "work which was in almost a defenceless condition, "and retired across the river to the town of "Bathurst. After this defeat, the chief of the "neighbouring Mahammedan towns, sent a large "contingent of men to the king of Barra; several "thousand armed natives were collected at a "distance of three miles only from Bathurst, and "the settlement was in such imminent danger "that the Lieut-Governor was compelled to send "to Sierra Leone for assistance.

" On November 9th the reinforcements "arrived in the Gambia and found Fort Bullen "still in the hands of the natives, who fortunately "had confined themselves to making mere "demonstrations instead of falling upon the

1831. Capture of Fort Bullen.

"settlement which lay entirely at their mercy. "On the morning of 11th November, a landing "was effected at Barra Point by the force con-"sisting of 451 of all ranks, under cover of a "heavy fire from H.M. brig "*Plumper*" (Lieut. "Cresey) the "*Parmalia*" transport, and an "armed colonial schooner. The enemy estimated "at from 2,500 to 3,000 strong, were skilfully "covered from the fire of the shipping by the "entrenchments which they had thrown up, and "from which as well as from the shelter of the "dense bush and high grass they poured in a "heavy and well sustained fire upon the troops "who were landing in the front.

" Notwithstanding all disadvantages, how-"ever, the British pushed on, and after an hour's "hard fighting during which the enemy con-"tested every inch of ground, they succeeded in "driving them from their entrenchments at the "point of the bayonet, and pursued them for "some distance through the bush. The British "loss in this action was two killed and three "officers (Captain Berwick, R.A.C., Lieut. "Lardner, 2nd West India and Captain Hughes, "Gambia Militia) and 47 men wounded.

" The next few days were occupied in "landing the guns and placing Fort Bullen in a "state of defence, and at daybreak on the morning "of November 17th the entire force marched to "the attack of Essaw, the king's town, leaving the "crew of H.M. brig "*Plumper*," under Lieut. Cresey "in charge of Fort Bullen.

" On approaching the vicinity of the town "the troops deployed into line, and the guns "having been brought to the front, a heavy fire "was opened on the stockades. This was kept "up for five hours, and was as vigorously returned

1831. Capture of Fort Bullen.

" by the enemy from their defences, with artillery " and small arms.

" The rockets were brought to bear as soon " as possible, and the first one thrown set fire to a " house in the town: but the buildings being prin- " cipally composed of "swish," and the natives " having taken the precaution of removing the " thatched roofs of the greater number, the rockets " produced but little effect as they could do no " harm to the walls.

" Towards noon some of the enemy were " observed leaving the rear of the town, and " shortly afterwards a very superior force of natives " appeared in the bush on the British right, " threatening an attack in flank, a second body " was also observed making a lengthened detour " to the left, apparently with the intention of " attacking the British rear. The men's am- " munition being almost exhausted, and the " artillery fire although well sustained having pro- " duced no effect upon the strong stockades, " which surrounded the town, it was deemed " prudent to retire, and the force was accordingly " withdrawn to Benty Point, having suffered " during the day 11 killed and 59 wounded. Lieut. " Leigh of the Sierra Leone Militia, and 5 men " subsequently died of their wounds."

On the 7th December reinforcements having arrived from Sierra Leone, the King of Barra notified his wish to open negociations. The British terms being accepted, a treaty was signed on the 4th January, 1832, and the troops returned to Sierra Leone.

Lieut. Lardner was twice wounded by a musket ball through the left arm on the 11th, and one through the left thigh on the 18th November,

1831. for which he received one year's pay from the War Office, and was mentioned as follows in despatches:

"The conduct of officers and men under "his command on this occasion was highly praise-"worthy, and particularly Lieut. Lardner of the "2nd West India Regiment, who although he was "severely wounded in the action of the 11th, "bravely led on the discharged soldiers with un-"daunted courage in the attack on the town on "the 17th."

1832. Bahamas.

In May, 1832, the Head-quarters and Grenadier company left Honduras for Bahamas, leaving the left wing at the former station. No further move took place until 1839.

Lieut.-Col. Pattison died. 1835.

Lieut.-Colonel A. Hope Pattison died at Nassau on 11th January, 1835.

1836.

In 1836 the establishment of lieut.-colonels was raised to two.

Fire at Belize in 1838.

On the 28th February an extensive fire broke out in Belize, which, except for the exertions of the troops, would have been most disastrous. "At "a meeting of the inhabitants held at the Court "House, Belize, on the 4th March, 1838, the fol-"lowing resolution was passed—

"Mr. W. Williamson moved, and was sec-"onded by Mr. Kennedy, that the thanks of this "meeting be voted to the Major (Anderson) com-"manding, officers, non-commissioned officers, and "privates of the 2nd West India Regiment, and also "of the Royal Artillery for the exertions made by them

Fire at Belize in 1838. "in suppressing on the night of the 28th ultimo, a "fire which threatened the destruction of this "town.

" By order of the Chairman,
" (Signed) PATRICK WALKER,
" Acting Keeper of Records."

In detachment orders, 13th March, Major Anderson published the above, and in paragraph 2 "Major Anderson has also much pleasure in "making known that Her Majesty's Superinten- "dent, the Colonel commanding, has expressed his "very high approbation of the conduct of the "officers, non-commissioned officers and men, as "coming under his own observation: and has fur- "ther received the commands of the Colonel com- "manding to make known to Lieut. Whitfeild and "Ensign Anderson his high sense of their exertions "in particular, and to assure those officers that he "will not fail to submit them in the most marked "manner to the General-Commanding-in-Chief."

1839. Jamaica. Two companies from Nassau, and two from Honduras, were sent to Jamaica, and formed the left wing in April; and in August, the head-quarters moved from Nassau to Jamaica, arriving in Spanishtown on the 11th.

The following officers accompanied head-quarters :—

Lieut.-Colonel W. B. Nicholls (in command) Major Anderson, Captain Allen, Lieut. and Adjutant Potts, Qr.-Mr. Harpur.

On the 13th December, 1841, head-quarters moved from Spanishtown to Up Park Camp; Major Allen commanding.

At the end of December, 1841, Major-General Sir W. Gomm handed over the command

1841. Jamaica. of troops in Jamaica to Major-General S. H. Berkeley, and, prior to doing so, issued the following General Order :—

General Order by Maj.-Gen. Sir W. Gomm.

" Jamaica, 25th December, 1841.
" . . . . And he would be greatly failing in "what is due to the portions of the 2nd and 3rd "West India Regiments stationed in this island, "did he neglect this opportunity of expressing his "sense of their great value in the command, of "their general good conduct and temperate habits "in quarters. Their readiness and activity from "time to time in the performance of those duties "which the heat of the climate renders onerous "under the same circumstances to their comrades, "the white soldiers, and their trustworthy behaviour "generally, which has enabled the Major-General "to relieve the European troops in stations where "their health has been most seriously affected, and "placed those important posts in the charge of the "black troops, upon whom experience has shewn "the climate not to have such prejudicial influence: "on all these accounts, the Major-General begs the "commanding officers of both corps in the island "—Major Allen and Captain Jackson—to accept "and convey from him to their men his warmest "acknowledgment.

" (Signed) W. Turner,
" Dep.-Adjt.-General."

1842. In January, 1842, a serious disturbance amongst the civil population took place in Kingston and a large body of troops were called out in aid of civil power; not only troops from near Kingston, but also from Newcastle and Port Royal. Sir William Gomm, although he had handed over the command and was still in the island, expressed his approval in a letter to Major-General Berkeley, which approval the general officer commanding was pleased to publish in the following order :—

1842. General Order by Maj.-Gen. Berkeley.

"General Orders, Jamaica, 12th January, 1842.

" Major-General Sir W. Gomm having made " the following communication to the M.-General " commanding, he feels great satisfaction in " promulgating the same in General Orders, as a " gratifying mark of the highly creditable conduct " of the troops employed, and he trusts that the " approbation of so distinguished an officer will " stimulate all ranks to persevere in adherence to " the system of discipline and regularity which has " obtained for them this satisfactory expression of " Sir William Gomm's favourable opinion.

Sir W. Gomm's Message.

" Having so recently taken occasion to " express my sense of the services and merits of " the departments and corps in the command, " preparatory to delivering them over to your " hands, it only remains for me further to express " to you my high satisfaction with the conduct of " such departments and corps as have been called " upon to take part in quelling the disturbances " in the city of Kingston, an emergency which has " arisen since the issue of my farewell order.

" These corps have consisted of the greater " portions of the 2nd and 3rd West India " Regiments in the command, a detachment Royal " Artillery, from Port Royal, and the 60th Rifles " from Newcastle.

" The West India Corps have behaved " throughout with the same steadiness and willing " obedience to orders I have ever found them " remarkable for.

" (Signed) W. Gomm, Major-General."

In 1840, the " Royal African Corps " was changed into the " 3rd West India Regiment "— the old 3rd West India had been disbanded in

1842. West African Garrison. 1819. This newly-named regiment remained—together with the recruiting companies, 1st and 2nd West India—as the garrison of the west coast of Africa until 1843; and in 1844, the head-quarters of the 3rd West India moved to the Bahamas, leaving one company at Sierra Leone, and one at the Gambia—two companies 2nd West India arriving there also, some time in 1843; while two companies of the 1st, and one company of the 3rd West India formed the garrison of Sierra Leone, the total garrison on the west coast being six companies.

1843. Jamaica. On the 25th August, 1843, there were some extensive fires in Kingston, and the regiment was called upon to give assistance. On the 28th, Major-General Berkeley addressed the following letter to Lieut.-Colonel Nicholls, commanding the regiment:—

" . . . . . The Major-General requests to " express, in this manner, to Lieut.-Colonel " Nicholls, commanding 2nd West India Regiment, " and Capt. Pack of the same corps, commanding " at Kingston Barracks, his full approbation of the " prompt and energetic, and judicious manner in " which the corps, under their command, were con- " ducted to and employed at the various situations " where their services were required, and efficiently " exerted during the continuance of those awful " fires which took place in different parts of the " City of Kingston on Saturday last.

" These officers will be pleased to convey " to the officers, non-commissioned officers and " soldiers under their command, assurance of the " Major-General's approval of their conduct, and " of his own sense of the cheerfulness, activity, and " well-directed exertions, evinced by them during " a protracted and laborious period of severe " fatigue."

1844. Jamaica. Death of Lieut.-Col. Nicholls.

Lieut.-Colonel Nicholls died on the 25th of May, 1844, at Up Park Camp, aged 63, having served in the Army a few days less than 49 years, the last twenty years having been passed with the regiment, leaving, amongst other sons, two serving in the regiment. Major Cobbe succeeded to the vacancy, and Captain Mends to the Majority.

1845. Headquarters to Nassau.

In March, the head-quarters under command of Captain H. W. Whitfeild, consisting of Grenadier and Light Companies, embarked for Nassau in the transport "*Princess Royal*," relieving the 3rd, and relieved by the 1st West India—leaving a detachment of four companies, Nos. 1, 6, 7 and 8 at Jamaica.

On the 12th of April, Lieut.-Colonel Cobbe arrived from England, and assumed command of the regiment.

1846.

Two companies (Nos. 7 and 8) joined headquarters at Nassau, on the 5th of February, 1846, in the transport "*Princess Royal*," from Jamaica, under command of Captain Fitzgerald, and the following letter was addressed to Lieut.-Colonel Cobbe :—

" Jamaica, 5th February, 1846.

" Sir,

" I am directed by the Lieut.-General "commanding to express to you his great satis-"faction at the correct and praiseworthy manner "in which the detachment of the 2nd West India "Regiment have uniformly performed their various "duties whilst under his command for a consider-"able period, as well as for their regular and "soldier-like conduct upon all occasions, whether "in quarters or otherwise.

1846. Nassau. "It has been a pleasing part of the Lieut.-"General's duty on more than one occasion to "have to report to His Grace the Commander-in-"Chief, the opinion he now expresses of the 2nd "West India Regiment.

"I have, &c.,

"(Signed) P. FARQUHARSON, Lieut.-Col., D.A.G.

"To officer commanding 2nd W.I. Regiment."

February. The regiment was now distributed as follows:—Head-quarters and 4 companies at Nassau, 2 companies at Jamaica and 2 companies at the Gambia.

1847. New Colours. New colours were provided for the regiment by the Colonel, Lieut.-General John Maister, and were presented at Nassau by Mrs. Anderson, wife of Major Anderson, late of the regiment, on the 23rd of September, 1847.

On the 28th of December, 1847, Nos. 1 and 6 companies embarked (under command of Major Soden) on H.M.S. "*St. Vesuvius*" for Trinidad and St. Lucia respectively.

The following General Orders were published on this occasion:—

General Orders No. 794.

"Jamaica, 27th of December, 1847.

"The Detachment of the 2nd West India "Regiment, under Major Soden being about to "embark for the Windward and Leeward Islands, "Major-General Lambert cannot allow them to "take their departure without expressing his satis-"faction in their general good conduct during the "time they have been under his command,

1847. Jamaica. "especially those stationed at Kingston Barracks "whose orderly behaviour he has had constant "opportunities of observing.

" (Signed) P. FARQUHARSON, Lieut.-Col, D.A.G."

1848. Headquarters to Spanishtown

On the 10th of March, 1848, the head-quarters and grenadier company under Lieut.-Colonel Cobbe, moved to Jamaica in hired transport "*Mary Irvine*," arriving at Spanishtown on the 10th.

Called out in aid of Civil Power.

On the 26th of August a part of the Grenadier company was sent in aid of civil power to St. Mary's returning to headquarters on 28th of September.

The following letter was received by the officer commanding troops, and forwarded to Major Mends, commanding the head-quarters:—

" King's House, 10th October, 1848.

"Sir,

" I am directed to say that if His Ex-"cellency the Governor had not been suffering "from his recent accident so as to be scarcely able "to transact the most urgent portion of the public "business, His Excellency would not have "deferred so long the expression of the sense His "Excellency entertains of the services of the "detachment of the 2nd West India Regiment, "under Captain Elliott, which was stationed for "some weeks in St. Mary's parish.

" At the time when the Governor applied for "military assistance there was every evidence for "apprehension that there would be determined "resistance of the police force by the small land-"holders of the negro class in the Goschen district, "and that it was impossible to calculate how

1848. Jamaica.

"widely the disturbance might spread; but from "the time of Captain Elliott's appearance in the "parish with his officers and detachment of 60 "men of the 2nd West India Regiment, tran- "quility and a sense of security appear to have "been restored, and the whole of the disputes and "differences have been referred to the arbitration "of the courts of law without the necessity of "having recourse to arms, or to any forcible "execution of legal process. The Governor "attributes this happy issue of affairs mainly to "the prudence and meritorious conduct of the "military, and especially to the steady and "judicious conduct of the officer in command.

" Not a single complaint against one of the "detachments has been made, either on the line of "march or in the neighbourhood of the estate "where the troops were stationed for several "weeks. The utmost harmony appears to have "prevailed between the officers and the resident "magistrate and gentry of the parish, and a grate- "ful feeling for the assistance and an approbation "of the exemplary discipline of the troops has "been very prevalent in all quarters.

" (Signed) CHARLES GREY,

" Lieut. R.A., Mil. Secretary."

On the 24th of September, 1848, Nos. 7, 8 and light infantry companies joined head-quarters from Nassau.

Chapter VII.

1848. Relief of Gambia Detachment

On the 21st of October No. 7 and 8 companies, under command of Lieut. Child, proceeded in transport "*Baretto Junior*" to the Gambia, relieving Nos. 3 and 4 companies, which arrived at Jamaica on the 15th of March, 1849.

1848-1849. West Africa Keenung Expedition.

On the 11th of April, 1849, Nos. 2 and 5 companies moved from Honduras to Granada and Tobago respectively.

May.

In May, the companies stationed at the Gambia took part in an expedition against the King of Keenung, Island of Basio, some 80 miles up the River Gambia.

1848-49. Keenung Expedition.

The expedition was composed of the following:—

	Capts.	Lieuts.	R. & F.
2nd W.I.....	1	4	149
3rd ,, ...	....	2	72
Enrolled Pensioners	1	....	40
Royal Gambia Volunteers	1	2	34
Total	3	8	295

The following were the officers of the 2nd West India Regiment engaged:—Captain S. J. Hill, Lieuts. McCourt, Child, Ayton and McLaughlin. The other officers of the expedition were Captain Grange, 1st West India, Commanding Pensioners; H. E. Captain McDonnell, commanding Volunteers; Lieut. Ireland, commanding Field Battery; Lieut. Hartigan, 3rd West India; Lieuts. Evans and Degrigney, Royal Gambia Volunteers; Assistant Staff-Surgeons Kekoe and Marchant; Assistant Commissary-General, Le Mesurer, Deputy Assistant Commissary-General Bell.

The casualties, 5 killed and 21 wounded; also 6 horses killed. Of these the 2nd West India lost 2 privates killed, 1 lieut. (McLaughlin), 2 company serjeant-majors (Beek and McKenzie), and 9 privates wounded—Captain Hill's horse was killed.

On the return of the expedition the merchants of the Gambia made the following address to Captain Hill, 2nd West India Regiment, commanding the forces:—

1849. Keenung. Expedition.

" Bathurst, Gambia, 30th May, 1849.

" Sir,

" We, the undermentioned British merchants and inhabitants of Bathurst, have unfeigned pleasure in tendering you our sincere thanks for the able and masterly manner in which you conducted the military operation with a very small force under your command against the King of Keenung, and to the officers who so ably supported you. We are fully sensible of the difficulties against which you had to contend. Unaided, as you were, by a naval force, and with only 264 rank & file (including officers), you landed in the enemy's country, marched inland a distance of 8 or 10 miles, carried by storm and utterly destroyed the town Bambucko, then marching on to the King's town of Keenung; you there inflicted such lasting punishment as we feel assured will not readily be forgotten by the natives, and you were only induced to desist from further operations on learning that the king and chiefs (the principal delinquents) had fled from the town, and on His Excellency the Governor acquainting you that he considered that the natives had been sufficiently punished.

Storming of Bambucko.

" It is true, sir, that as British soldiers, you may say you and the officers under your command have only performed your duty—to do which is no doubt the just and proud ambition of every soldier; we too feel a high gratification in bearing testimony to your having done so, most gallantly and efficiently, and in maintaining the high character of the British arms.

" We cannot forget that former expeditions, which the local government here has before been obliged to have recourse to, in order to punish unprovoked aggressions on the part of the natives, have failed in their objects, although attempted

1849. Keenung Expedition

"with much larger forces, and assisted in their "transport by the boats of vessels of war—an "advantage of which you were deprived, and "which would have added much to the strength of "your little force.

" We feel, therefore, to your cool, per- "sonal determination and indomitable courage "in command, as well as to the personal bravery "and daring of the officers under you, and who "were more than usually exposed, that we are so "largely indebted for the termination successfully "of the expedition, thereby teaching the natives "that the local government is able to protect, and "punish their wanton acts of aggression. We "sincerely hope that Her Majesty's Government "at home will be pleased to appreciate the good "services you have rendered to the colony by "conferring upon you some distinguishing mark of "their approbation. No official notification of the "proceedings of the expedition having been "published, we have been obliged to delay this "expression of our sentiments until now to enable "us to get authentic information of the impression "made upon the natives; and we are happy in "being able to express the hope that the effect of "your achievements will be to instil a high moral "lesson upon the native chiefs throughout the "river that will teach them the necessity of "respecting British lives and property when "peacefully engaged in commerce amongst them.

" Sincerely wishing you every success in life "we have the honour to be, sir, your obedient "and humble servants,

" (Signed) James J. Davis,
" W. W. Goddard,
" T. J. S. Tender,
" And 21 more."

1849. Keenung Expedition. The following extract from a letter dated Bathurst, 16th June, 1849, from Captain Hill to the *Naval and Military Gazette* is interesting :—

" We suffered severely from the intense heat " of the climate—thermometer 130°—and the " scorching air from the burning towns was in- " tolerable. We were constantly engaged for " three successive days against an enemy numer- " ically superior at ten to one, and for want of " sufficient transport had to take the field without " tents, and bivouacked in the open air exposed to " the heavy dews of this country.

" The enemy, it has been ascertained as a " fact, lost between 3,000 and 4,000 *hors de* " *combat.*"

The following complimentary letters were received in reference to the " Keenung Expedition."

" Government House, Bathurst.
December 1st, 1849.

" Sir,

" I have lately received from the Right " Honourable the Secretary of State for the " Colonies a despatch expressing his Lordship's " views in reference to the expedition undertaken " last May against the King of Keenung.

" In that despatch his Lordship informs me " (par. 7) that he has expressed to the Commander- " in-Chief of Her Majesty's Army the opinion " which he entertains, that the Officer in command " of the troops acted with great judgment and " intrepidity, during those operations.

" Such a high testimony of your merit must " be most gratifying to a soldier like yourself, who " looks on the approbation of those, whose approval

1849. Keenung Expedition. "is an honour, as the greatest reward he can obtain "for any exertions he may be called upon to make, "in the cause of his arduous but honourable "profession.

" Permit me to add that on my own part I "feel especially gratified at conveying the above "approval of Her Majesty's Government to an "Officer who both in private and official life has "honourably exerted himself since his assumption "of the command here, to render every assistance "in his power to the community and the executive, "and who by his cheerful and indefatigable dis-"charge of every duty entrusted to him, has "entirely deserved and obtained the confidence of "myself as Governor.

" I have &c.,
" (Signed) RICHARD GRAVES MACDONALD,
" Governor and Commander-in-Chief.
"To the Honourable
" Captain Hill, 2nd W.I. Regt.
" Commanding Troops.

1849. Cage Coote Expedition. In December, 1849, a British Schooner "*Grant*" was seized by pirates and a joint Naval and Military Expedition under the command of Commodore Fanshawe proceeded to the Island of Basio, Seba River.

The following details embarked on H.M. steamer "*Teazer*" about the 10th December—

2nd W.I. Regt., 1 Capt. (Hill), 2 lieuts. (McCourt and McLoughton), 50 non-commissioned officers and men.

3rd W.I. Regt., 15 non-commissioned officers and men, the whole under command of Capt. Hill. The pirates were attacked and defeated on the 12th and the schooner recovered.

1849. **Cage Coote Expedition.**

Captain Hill received a Brevet Majority for this service.

The following flattering correspondence in reference to this action took place.

"Horse Guards, 5th February, 1850.

" Sir,

" I have the honour to receive your letter of "the 24th December last, transmitting for the "information of the Commander-in-Chief, a copy " of your despatch to Governor Macdonald, respect- " ing the proceedings of a detachment under your "command, embarked to assist the Naval " Commander-in-Chief on the African station in "recovery of a British schooner, captured by " pirates, who murdered the master and a large " part of the crew about 200 miles down the coast "South of the Gambia ; as also a copy of His " Excellency's reply with a copy of Commodore " Fanshawe's letter to him, approving of the " manner in which the troops had performed their "duty.

" Having laid these papers before the Duke " of Wellington, I have much satisfaction in "acquainting you that His Grace has perused "your report with the greatest pleasure and is " most happy to learn that the officers and men of "the 2nd and 3rd West India Regiments con- " ducted themselves in so gallant a manner under " very trying circumstances.

" I am instructed to forward to you a copy " of a letter I have received from the Admiralty " transmitting (to be laid before the Commander- "in-Chief) the extract of one from Captain Buckle "of H.M. steamer '*Centaur*' bearing testimony to "the aid afforded by you and the detachment " under your orders, and requesting that the thanks

1849. Cage Coote Expedition.

"of their Lordships may be conveyed to you and "them, for your and their efficient co-operation on "the occasion.

"It is highly gratifying to the duke, this "communication, to make to you.

"I have &c.,
"(Signed) FITZROY SOMERSET.

"Capt. Hill, 2nd W.I. Regt.,
"Commanding the troops.

Enclosure No. 1.

"Admiralty, 31st January, 1850.

Thanks of the Lords of the Admiralty.

"My Lord,
"I am commanded by my Lord Commis- "sioners of the Admiralty to send you herewith for "the information of His Grace the Commander-in- "Chief, an extract from a letter from Captain "Buckle of H.M.S. '*Centaur*,' dated 13th December "last, bearing testimony to the aid afforded by a "detachment of the 2nd West India Regiment "under command of Captain Hill, which had "assisted in the recovery of the British schooner "'*Grant*,' seized by pirates on the West Coast of "Africa; and I am to request that His Grace will "cause the thanks of their lordships to be "conveyed to Captain Hill and the men under his "orders, for their aid and co-operation, on the "occasion.

"I have &c.

"(Signed) J. PARKER,

"To Lieut.-General
"Lord Fitzroy Somerset, G.C.B., &c., &c.

1849.
Cage Coote Expedition.

Enclosure 2.

Extract from a letter from Captain Buckle to the Admiralty, dated H.M.S. "*Centaur*" 6 miles north of Kellet Island, Balanter Bay, 13th December, 1849.

" It is with much satisfaction that I have " now to report the steady determined conduct, " and cheerful endurance of all employed in the " expedition.

" My best thanks are due to Captain Hill, " commanding the detachment of the gallant 2nd " West India Regiment, he was always in advance, " and I received much advantage from his ex- " perience, and advice; and the steady determined " bearing of himself, his officers, and men, was " most apparent."

Captain Hill to be Bt. Major for his services.

" Horse Guards, February 8th, 1850.

" Sir,

" Referring to my letter of the 5th inst., I " have now the honour to transmit to you a copy " of a letter from the under Secretary of State, " conveying the extract of a despatch from the " Governor H.M's Settlement on the Gambia and " its enclosure, and expressing Earl Grey's " approbation of your conduct, and that of the " detachment under your command, in the " expedition to which the papers refer, and I have " at the same time the greatest satisfaction in " adding that the Commander-in-Chief proposes " as a mark of his approbation of your services " immediately to submit to the Queen that you " should be promoted to the rank of Major by " Brevet,

" I have &c.,

" (Signed) FITZROY SOMERSET.

" To Capt. Hill, 2nd W.I. Regiment.

1849.
Keenung Expedition.

" Horse Guards, July 27th, 1850.
" Sir,
" I have to acknowledge the receipt of your " letter of the 19th inst., enclosing a copy of a " letter addressed to you by the Governor of the " Gambia Settlements, dated 18th April, 1850, and " expressive of your hope that 'the Commander-" in-Chief considers you acted fully up to the spirit " of your instructions when conducting the " military expedition last May into the interior " against the King of Keenung, and soliciting " some mark of approval' and having duly laid " the same before the Commander-in-Chief, I " have to acquaint you that His Grace has seen " with satisfaction that your performance of that " duty manifested the same zeal, intelligence and " gallantry as upon the later occasion, when " commanding in December 1849, an expedition " against the natives of a place called Cage Coote, " and for which service Her Majesty was graciously " pleased to confer upon you the Brevet rank of " Major.

" I have &c.,

" (Signed) FITZROY SOMERSET.

" To
" Brevet Major Hill, 2nd W.I. Regt., &c.

Chapter VIII.

1850.
West India Moves.

No. 3 and 4 companies embarked at Port Royal under command of Lieut.-Colonel Faber on the 9th March, 1850, on the transport "*Princess Royal*" and were conveyed to St. Kitts and Dominica respectively.

1851.
Headquarters Demerara.

Headquarters (Grenadiers and Light Company) embarked on board H.M. steamer "*Inflexible*" on the 13th February, 1851, and landed at Demerara on the 25th March, under command of Lieut.-Colonel Cobbe.

1852.
Nos. 1, 2, 5, 6 Companies joined Headquarters.

On the 17th March, 1852, No. 2 Company joined head-quarters from Grenada, and on 25th July H.M. troopship "*Megæra*" disembarked No. 5 Company from Tobago; No. 1 Company from Trinidad and No. 6 Company from St. Lucia.

On the 25th May, 1853, H.M. troopship "*Megæra*" embarked the Grenadiers and No. 2 Company at Demerara, and conveyed them to Trinidad and Jamaica respectively.

1853. West Indies Moves.

No. 4 Company commanded by Captain Mends embarked at Dominica in June and was conveyed in the same ship to Jamaica.

African Relief. No. 7 & 8 Companies to Headquarters.

This year (1853) the quintennial relief of the West African Garrison took place—Nos. 7 and 8 Companies arrived at Demerara on 22nd July, on board H.M. troop ship "*Resistance*" from the West Coast, under command of Ensign Burleigh, and Nos. 1 and 6 Companies under command of Captain Mockler and Ensign Inman, embarked on the following day (23rd July) and were distributed as follows:—

No. 1 & 6 Companies to Africa.

No. 1 company at Sierra Leone, No. 6 company at the Gambia.

No. 3 company proceeded to Tortola in aid of civil power on the 2nd August, 1853, and joined head-quarters at Demerara on the 27th February, 1855.

Storming of Sabbajee Nos. 7 & 8 Companies.

Before the companies (Nos. 7 and 8) were relieved at the Gambia, they were engaged in the suppression of a hostile movement amongst the Mohammedans at Sabbajee. Advantage was taken of the troopship *Resistance* arriving from the West Indies with two companies of the 1st West India, in relief of two others. The force at the Gambia now temporally consisting of two companies 1st, two companies 2nd, and one company 3rd West India; the total strength being 463 effective; in addition to this there were 35 pensioners, and 105 of the Gambia Militia; two six-pounder field guns and two howitzers. The following is an extract from Ellis' History—1st West India Regiment:—

"On the 30th May, the Brigade marched "from Bathurst to Josswung, a distance of eight

1853. Storming of Sabbajee Nos. 7 & 8 Companies.

"miles, where a camp was formed, and on the 1st "June the force advanced to the attack of "Sabbajee.

"Sabbajee was one of the oldest Marabout "towns in Combo, and possessed the largest "mosque in that portion of Africa.

"The town, more than a mile in circum-"ference, was surrounded by a strong stockade, "double ditches and outward abattis, and the "inhabitants, who could muster 3,000 fighting men, "were, from their predatory and war-like habits, "the dread of the surrounding country.

"On approaching the town, a strong body "of the enemy was observed stationed round the "mosque, while the stockade presented the "appearance of having been removed, but had, in "reality, only been laid lengthwise, so as to form a "very formidable obstacle; while a deep trench in "rear was crowded with men, who could, in perfect "security, fire on the advancing British, should "they fall into the trap which had been laid for "them, and attempt to carry the town at this "point.

"The force was drawn up in three divisions, "the 1st West India Regiment, under Captain "Murray, forming the centre division, the 2nd "West India Regiment, under Captain Anderson, "the right, and the 3rd West India Regiment, "under Captain Brabazon, the left. At about 400 "yards from the stockade, the field battery opened "fire, and with such precision, that after a few "rounds, the roof of the mosque, and those of the "adjacent houses, were in flames; observing the "disorder caused amongst the enemy by the "burning of their sacred building, Lieut.-Colonel

1853. Storming of Sabbajee Nos. 7 & 8 Companies.

" O'Connor determined to seize the opportunity " and storm.

" The right and left divisions extended in " skirmishing order, the centre remaining in " column, and the whole advanced to the assault.

" The enemy kept up a heavy fire from the " loopholes of their stockade, over which the green " flag was flying, but, at the same moment, the " three divisions, which had in advancing formed a " crescent, rushed at the stockade at three different " points, and, clambering over, got at the enemy " with the bayonet. This was more than they " could stand, and, abandoning their stockade, " they fled down the streets and escaped through " sallyports in rear of the town.

" A strong body of fanatics, however, still " held the mosque, the fire in the roof of which " they had succeeded in extinguishing, and, amid " the beating of war-drums, and the cries of " 'Allah,' from the priests, kept up a smart fire " upon the troops as they entered the large central " square where the mosque stood. To have " stormed the building would have involved great " sacrifice of life; and the men, therefore, were " directed to occupy the houses enclosing the " square, and open fire until the rockets could be " brought into play.

" The second rocket whizzed through the " roof of the mosque, the defenders of which, " however, only increased their drumming and " shouts of defiance, for they were secure in their " belief of the local tradition, which said that the " mosque was impregnable and indestructible. In " a very few minutes, flames began to appear on " the roof, and, though the enemy worked hard to " extinguish it, it rapidly increased, until the

1853. Storming of Sabbajee.

" mosque was untenable. Dozens of fanatics blew " out their brains rather than surrender, while " others threw themselves out of the windows and " passages, and rushed sword in hand in a state of " frenzy upon the British. The coolness and " steadiness of the troops was, however, more than " a match for the mad rage of the Mandingoes, " who were shot down one after another, until the " whole of the defenders of the mosque were killed " or made prisoners. The remainder of the enemy, " who had fled at the storming of the stockade, " had taken refuge in the neighbouring woods, and " the object of the engagement being accomplished " by the capture of the town, they were not pur- " sued.

" The stockade and mosque being destroyed, " the force left Sabbajee on June 4th, and returned " to Joss-Wing, whereby an arrangement with the " King of Congo, a portion of that kingdom, " including the town of Sabbajee, was ceded to the " British."

The following officers of the 2nd W. I. Regiment took part in the expedition, *viz.*, Capt. Anderson, Lieuts. Drouet and Gordon-Grant.

1854. Honduras Nos. 2 & 4 Companies.

In 1854, Nos. 2 and 4 companies moved from Grenada and Dominica to Honduras, where they were stationed under command of Major Miller.

Great fire at Belize.

On the 18th July, a serious fire broke out at Belize: the detachment was called out, and very materially assisted in preventing the spread of the fire, and in the preservation of property; from the fact that all the houses in the town were built of wood, with shingle (wood) roofs, and raised off the ground on piles, which causes a current of air, and that at this time of the year, there is always a

1854. Belize.

strong breeze from the sea, it can be understood what determined exertion was necessary to save the town. One soldier lost his life, and many were seriously hurt.

A public meeting was convened, and the thanks of the community was accorded to officers and men of the detachment.

The following letter was received in reply to the official report of the occurrence:—

"Horse Guards,
" 22nd September, 1854.
" Sir,
" I have laid before the General-Commanding-" ing-in-Chief your letter of the 24th ultimo, " containing amongst other enclosures, the order " issued by Major Miller, 2nd West India " Regiment, on the occasion of the recent fire at " Belize, and the thanks given to that officer, and " the troops engaged under him, by the Council of " Honduras, and am directed to acquaint you that " it has been very gratifying to his Lordship to " peruse the testimony borne to the good conduct " of the troops on that occasion.
" Viscount Hardinge, however, regrets with " you the loss of Lance-Corporal William Maturin, " 2nd West India Regiment, who died from the " effect of a severe burn.
" I have, &c.,
" (Signed) G. A. WETHERALL,
" To Major-General D.A.G.
" Sir Richard Doherty,
" &c., &c., Jamaica."

Affairs in Africa.

In September, 1854, the natives of Accra rebelled against British authority, and drove the Gold Coast Artillery, which then formed the garrison of the Gold Coast, into the castle at

1854. Relief of Christiansborg Nos. 1 & 6 Companies.

Christiansborg, which they invested. On information being received at Sierra Leone, a force, under command of Captain Rookes, 2nd West India Regiment, was despatched to the relief of the castle. The details composing this force consisted of—1st West India—Lieut. Strachan, Ensign Anderson, and 58 non-commissioned officers and men.

2nd West India—Captains Rookes and Mockler, and 116 non-commissioned officers and men.

3rd West India—Lieuts. Haneahan and Hill, and 54 non-commissioned officers and men.

Total strength—six officers and 228 non-commissioned officers and men.

This force arrived at Christiansborg in two detachments, on the 27th October and 7th November respectively, but on its appearance, the rebels retired inland and dispersed. The troops embarked for Sierra Leone on the 12th November, arriving there on the 25th.

No sooner had the troops arrived at Sierra Leone, from the Gold Coast, than fresh work was found to be awaiting them.

1854. Malageah Expedition. December, 1854. Nos. 1 & 6 Companies.

In consequence of the outrages committed by the natives in the neighbourhood of the Mellicourie and Scarcies rivers, it was determined by the authorities to despatch a punitive expedition against the Chief of Malageah, and the following force, under command of Captain Rookes, were detailed for this duty:

1st Division—1st W. I.—Captain Fletcher, Lieuts. Connell & Strachan, and Ensign Anderson;

1854. Malageah Expedition. 2nd Division.—2nd W. I.—Captain Rookes (in command), Captain Mockler, Lieut. St. Aubyn, and Ensign Surman;

3rd Division.—3rd W. I.—Lieuts. Lamont and Hill;

Commissariat—D.A.C.G.s Winter, Frith, and O'Connor;

Medical.—Staff-Surgeon Marchant; Staff-Assistant-Surgeons Bradshaw and Hendley;

384 non-commissioned officers and men of the West India regiments.

The force embarked on board H.M.S. *Dover* and H.M.S. *Prometheus* on the 2nd December, and arrived off the town of Malageah on the 4th.

Before disembarking, the following orders were issued by Captain Rookes:—

" H.M.S. *Prometheus*,
" December 4th, 1854, (7 a.m.)
" The troops will be prepared to disembark " at 10 o'clock in the following order:

" The division of the 2nd West India " Regiment, under command of Captain Mockler, " will, after landing, form in front of the town, " having been previously told off into com- " panies on board ship, and will, when ordered, " proceed to attack the King's house, on the hill, " near the mosque.

December 4th, 1854. Capture of Malageah " The 3rd West India will act as support to " the advance, under Captain Mockler, leaving a " strong guard at the landing place.

" The 1st West India Regiment, under " command of Captain Fletcher, will proceed in

Dec. 1854.
Malageah Expedition.
Nos. 1 & 6 Companies.

"the pinnace of H.M.S. *Britomart*, and paddle-boat, "up the creek to the eastward of the town, and act "on landing as circumstances require."

The landing was unopposed, and after a little successful manœuvring, the town was captured. The force returned to Sierra Leone on the following day, arriving on the 6th, having accomplished its mission without a shot being fired, the King signing the required treaty, and paying one thousand dollars as a fine.

The following letters give a full account of this affair:—

No. 1.—" From O.C. troops, S. Leone;
" to Secretary of State for War.

" Sierra Leone, 9th December, 1854.
" My Lord Duke,
" The command of the troops on the West "Coast of Africa having devolved on me by the "death of Lieut.-Colonel Foster, 3rd West India "Regiment, and the absence of Lieut.-Colonel "O'Connor at Teneriffe, I have the honour to "acquaint you that immediately on return of the "expeditionary force under my command from the "Gold Coast, a requisition was made on the late "Lieut.-Colonel Foster, commanding, for a body "of troops to proceed in H.M. ships '*Prometheus*' "and '*Dover*' to the town of Malageah, on the "right bank of the river Mellicourie. Having "been nominated to command the force, I em- "barked on Saturday, the 2nd December, 401 "officers and men of all ranks, including the "commissariat and medical departments; on the "4th we arrived off the town of Malageah.

" On consulting with the senior naval officer, "Captain Heseltine, of the '*Britomart*,' who had

1854. Malageah Expedition.

"arrived, and commanded the '*Dover*,' and was "also the diplomatic agent, charged with nego-"tiating powers from the acting Governor of this "colony, it was considered advisable for us to "personally reconnoitre the positions for debarking. "Captain Selwyn, of the '*Prometheus*,' accom-"panied us.

" I enclose the order issued on the occasion, "which was carried out in all its details most "admirably by Captains Fletcher and Mockler.

" Although the enemy offered no opposition, "professing their readiness to submit to all de-"mands, yet knowing from experience the "treacherous nature of the natives: I resolved "upon the occupation of the town, and accordingly "directed an advance upon the mosque and King's "house, which was secured by the troops, as also "were all the avenues leading to them in our "possession ten minutes after landing.

" By this quick movement, I surrounded "about 150 to 200 of the chiefs and Maraboos, "who filled the interior of the mosque. Captain "Fletcher here joined me with the 1st division "from the landing on the eastern side of the town.

" After a halt of about an hour, seeing the "Maraboos gradually leaving the mosque in one "direction, I made a personal reconnaissance, at "the head of ten men, accompanied by my field-"adjutant—Lieut. Connell—and Dr. Bradshaw, "to the northern side of the town; on our arrival "at the town gate, I observed about 1,600 to 2,000 "natives, all completely armed with firelocks, "spears, and bows and arrows, formed in a half-"circle, and averaging from eight to ten deep. I "immediately despatched an officer to the rear, "and directed him to instruct Captain Fletcher to "bring up the whole of the main body, with sea-"men and marines, and, on their arrival, I

1854. Malageah Expedition.

"debouched upon the plateau, on which the enemy "was posted, and took up a position exactly in "their front, and about 15 yards from their centre. "I had previously directed the 3rd division (3rd "W. I. R.) to occupy the walls and gate of the "town in our rear, through which I had marched, "and keep up connecting files between them and "the ships; our right rested on the road to "Mallicourie, and our left commanded the road to "Fouricaria.

"At first there was a disposition to oppose "this movement; but it was so rapidly executed, "that before they were well aware of our presence, "our position was secure. I attribute the peace-"ful settlement of the affair entirely to the "admirable discipline and steadiness of the troops, "and to Captain Selwyn's tact and intimate "knowledge of the native character. Not a single "casualty occurred in any of their disembark-"ations or embarkations whilst under my "command, nor was there a case of drunkenness "or insubordination; and when it is considered "that the troops were untried, and whilst at Accra "(Gold Coast) and Malageah, immediately in the "presence of a crafty and cruel enemy, their "conduct was beyond all praise.

" (Signed) CHARLES ROOKES,
" Capt. 2nd W.I. Regt.,
"To His Grace Commanding Troops.
" The Duke of Newcastle,
" &c., &c., &c."

Letter No. 2.—" H.M.S. '*Britomart*,'
" Sierra Leone, December 6th, 1854.

"Sir,

"In bringing back the troops which have "been embarked on board the "*Prometheus*" and "landed at Malageah, and who whilst afloat have "have been under my command, I beg to bear

1854. Malageah Expedition.

"testimony to their quiet, orderly and zealous "conduct both afloat and on shore, where, had it "not been for the above good qualities, and the "forbearance of the officers, collision would have "been inevitable. To Captains Rookes (com- "manding), Mockler and Fletcher, and the "officers in the force, I beg to return my sincere "thanks for their zealous and active co-oper- "ations—further comment on my part would be "presumptuous.

" (Signed) A. HESELTINE.

" To Lieut-Col. Foster,
" Commanding the Troops,
" Commander and Senior Officer."

Letter No. 3.—" Mellicourie Town.

" Mellicourie River, 12th December, 1854.

" Sir,

" We, the undersigned French and English "merchants and traders in the Mellicourie River, "consider it a pleasing duty to convey to you as "the officer commanding the troops, who formed "in concert with H.M.S. '*Britomart*,' '*Prome- "theus*' and '*Dover*,' the late expedition to the "river, the gratifying expression of our thanks for "the great zeal evinced by yourself, Captains "Fletcher and Mockler, and the other officers and "men under your command, for the protection and "preservation of very much valuable property "belonging to us, and threatened with destruction, "in consequence of menaces held out against those "trading in the river by the king, Morifahi, and "other chiefs and headmen who had given them "notice to quit the river in ten days or abide the "consequences, alleging as their reason for thus "acting, certain aggressions on the part of the "Sierra Leone Government against their country- "people by seizure of canoes with slaves from the "Sherbro River.

1854. **Malageah Expedition.**

" The expedition having proceeded to " Malageah, the chief town and residence of " Morifahi, the troops under your command were " landed and drawn up upon the race-course ; this " we do not doubt, had a very great effect upon " that chief in inducing him to retract his obstinacy " and enter into negotiations with Captain Hesel- " tine of H.M.S. '*Britomart*,' which resulted, " happily, without loss of life, in the restoration of " tranquility to the river, and to a better state of " affairs in it, which, it must be hoped, may prove " permanent. Without wishing to derogate from " the merits of the naval portion of the expedition, " we consider the appearance of efficiency and the " orderly behaviour of the troops under your " command contributed very materially towards " the desirable end. Reiterating our best thanks " to yourself, Captains Fletcher and Mockler, and " the other officers under your command, and " expressing a wish for your and their health " during your service upon the trying coast of " Africa and success in your profession,

" We beg to remain, &c., &c.,

" (Signed) B. H. DAVISON,
" A. VALENTINE-DEEPYS,
" And 7 others.

" To Captain Rookes, 2nd W.I. Regiment,
" Commanding Troops, Sierra Leone."

Letter No. 4.

" From Military Secretary, Horse Guards,

" To Captain Rookes, Horse Guards,
" 7th March, 1855.

" Sir,

" Having had the honour to receive and " submit to the General-Commanding-in-Chief " your letter of the 2nd instant, enclosing copies " of two letters, the one from the French and

1854. Malageah Expedition.

"English merchants and traders of the river "Mellicourie, and the other from his Excellency "the Governor of Sierra Leone, conveying the "thanks for service rendered by the officers, non-"commissioned officers, and men, in the expedition "under your command.

" I am directed to acquaint you that his "Lordship is *much gratified* by the perusal of these "testimonials to the zeal evinced by yourself and "the other officers and men under your command "in the protection and preservation of property, "and to the judgment with which the operations "of the expedition were conducted by you.

" (Signed) C. YORK,
" Military Secretary.

"To Capt. Rookes, 2nd W.I. Regiment."

Captain Rookes also received the thanks of the Local Government in the following letter from Colonel Stephen Hill (Governor of Sierra Leone and the Gold Coast), dated Sierra Leone, 12th January, 1855:—

Extract.—"I also take this opportunity of "thanking you for the zealous and efficient sup-"port you rendered to the Government of the Gold "Coast whilst you were lately serving in command "of the Sierra Leone and Gambia reinforcements "at Accra during a very trying period, and when "I am aware both yourself, officers and men, had "to endure many privations consequent on the "disturbed state of the district.
" (Signed) STEPHEN J. HILL,
" Governor."

In May of this year a disastrous expedition to Malageah was undertaken, composed of 1st and 3rd West India. I consider some mention may

Up Park Camp, Jamaica.

1855. West Africa. Second Malageah Expedition.

well be made of this expedition in these records as, on the disbandment of the 3rd West India, a large number of officers and men were drafted into the 2nd West India, besides which an officer of the regiment took a prominent part in it.

It was decided by the acting Governor of Sierra Leone, who was the Queen's Advocate, and a coloured man, to destroy the town of Malageah, because the King had not paid the fine of one thousand dollars imposed after the previous expedition of December, 1854. With very little knowledge of what force was necessary to accomplish this, he insisted, contrary to the advice of the officer commanding troops, that what troops were stationed at Tower Hill, consisting of 150 all told, should be despatched that very day, instead of waiting a couple of days, by which time the detachment—2nd West India—could have been brought in from Waterloo, and a force of sufficient strength assembled.

The following is the official report of this affair :—

" Sierra Leone, 26th May, 1855.

" Sir,

" In pursuance of an order received from " your Excellency, dated 21st instant, I embarked " on board H.M. steamship '*Teazer*,' in command " of (150) one hundred and fifty men of all ranks " of the 1st and 3rd West India regiments, and " the undermentioned officers :—

" 1st W. I. Regt.—Lieuts. Strachan and Wylie;

" 2nd W. I. Regt.—Lieut. Vincent (attached to " 1st W. I. Regt.);

1855. Second Malageah Expedition.

"3rd W. I. Regt.—Lieuts. Kier and Beazley "(garrison adjutant);

"Medical Staff—2nd class Staff-Surgeon Marchant "and Staff-Asst.-Surgeon Bradshaw;

"Commissariat Dept.—Acting-Depy.-Asst.-Com.-"Gen. Frith.

" H.M.S. '*Teazer*' arrived at Benty-point, at "the mouth of the Mallicourie River, on the "morning of the 22nd instant. We were unable "to cross the bar: the tide not suiting, caused a "few hours' delay. We arrived at the town of "Malageah at 9 o'clock the same morning.

" The troops disembarked under cover of "the guns of the '*Teazer*,' and formed upon the "bank; the commander of the '*Teazer*,' and Mr. "Dillet soon after joined on shore.

" At the time of our landing, a flag of truce "was flying at the King's house, and on board the "'*Teazer*.' I consented, with the advice of the "two commissioners, Commander Nicolas of "H.M.S. '*Teazer*,' and Mr. Dillet above men-"tioned, to allow one hour to elapse before we "opened fire upon the town; after the lapse of "more than an hour-and-a-half, Commander "Nicolas returned on board, and opened with shell "and grape, to cover the troops, who immediately "commenced to advance with skirmishers thrown "out on either flank of the main division.

" We proceeded to the centre of the town, "and after setting fire to the mosque, King's house, "and several of the principal buildings, with the "aid of a small rocket party from the '*Teazer*,' it "appeared as if the whole town was in a blaze, we "then were obliged to retire to the boats on account

1855. Second Malageah Expedition.

"of the extreme heat of the burning houses, and "the probability of the troops suffering therefrom.

" Whilst we were embarking, a very sharp "fire was opened upon us from both sides of the "landing-place by the enemy in ambush, but I am "happy to state that only five of our men were "wounded.

" After the troops had all got on board, the "whole of the town being apparently in flames, it "was discovered that one portion of it had not "been burnt; upon that we consulted together and "determined to proceed as far as Benty-point that "evening, and on the following morning to return "and effectually reduce the whole of the place to "ashes, according to the instructions received to "that effect, being fully convinced of the import-"ance of that object.

" At half-past 5 o'clock a.m., on the 23rd, "we started from Benty, and anchored off the "town of Malageah, which was still in flames; the "'*Teazer*' then commenced shelling, throwing "grape occasionally into the bushes: after the "lapse of half-an-hour, the troops disembarked, "no enemy appearing in sight to resist our landing, "the men formed and advanced upon the town for "the purpose of setting fire to the parts still "standing.

" Commander Nicolas and Mr. Dillet went "on with the advance for the purpose of pointing "out the houses to be destroyed.

" The main division then prepared to cover "the advance: at this moment I observed them "driven back, having been suddenly attacked by "an overwhelming number of well-armed natives.

1855. Second Malageah Expedition.

"Mr. Dillet, captain of the Sierra Leone "Militia, and private secretary to your Excellency, "fell to the rear at this moment, and I observed "him wounded in the head and left leg.

"Commander Nicolas was, I regret, at the "same time, shot through both thighs, and Ser-"geant-Major Scanlan, 3rd West India Regiment, "was killed on the spot. The former I directed to "be taken on board, and sent Staff-Asst.-Surgeon "Bradshaw with him. I then ordered a part of "the main division forward and accompanied them "leaving Lieut. Keir (3rd West India Regiment) "with instructions to prevent our rear being cut "off. He was obliged to sound one division to "retire as the enemy had almost surrounded us, "and cut us off. The men were falling fast, and "the enemy pressed upon us in all directions, and "one of the seamen of the "*Teazer*" was struck "in the stomach by a war club, after having been "wounded in the arm (named John Hill). Myself, "Lieut. Wylie of the 1st West India Regiment "(whom, I regret to add, is killed) Lieut. Vincent "of the 2nd West India Regiment, and about 18 "or 20 men were driven back upon a small island "of mud and sand upon the left side of the "entrance to the town of Malageah; a great "number of men were here shot, and Lieut. Vincent "of the 2nd West India Regiment was immediately "shot through the body; he showed his wound "to me and jumped into the water to swim to a "boat.

"After the troops had embarked, the largest "boat containing some 40 men suddenly filled and "capsized, having, as I afterwards learned, been "perforated with bullets.

"A flag of truce was then hoisted, which "I am grieved to say was not respected by the

1855. Second Malageah Expedition.

"enemy and to this cause I attribute the immense "loss of our men.

"Acting Dep.-Asst.-Com.-General Frith is "reported to having been taken prisoner.

"Of the officers composing the expedition-"ary force, I cannot speak too highly in their "praise, but as I consider it would be presump-"tuous on my part to comment on the conduct of "troops during an action in which one-half of the "men engaged were either killed or wounded, or "missing. I will say no further on the subject but "that I received the greatest assistance from every "officer who was present.

"By Lieut. Keir, 3rd West India Regiment, "second in command, by Lieut. Vincent, 2nd "West India Regiment, and my Field-Adjt. Lieut. "Beazley, 3rd West India Regiment, I was "afforded all the assistance I could have wished, "but in an action where every officer vied with "another in carrying out their duties to the "fullest extent it would be invidious on my part "to speak more in praise of one than another. . . .

"The whole of the shell and grape having "been expended, and the banks of the river lined "with armed men, the troops having embarked "(with the exception of those who sunk with the "pinnace, who were wounded or taken prisoners), "we proceeded slowly down the river, firing as we "retired after the refusal of the enemy to respect "the flag of truce, which was hoisted upon the "sinking of the boat.

"We took the Prime Minister (Marmados "Tray) prisoner, together with other valuable "spoil and one gun, but I must regret to add that "the action was attended with serious loss on our

1855. Second Malageah Expedition.

"side, which will be made known to your "Excellency in the enclosed report.

"After all had embarked, I escaped by "swimming to the "*Teazer*," and as I was close "upon her, was picked up by a boat and taken "on board.

"I trust your Excellency will observe that "we fully carried out our instructions, although "attended with the loss above alluded to.

" (Signed) R. D. FLETCHER, Capt. 1st W.I.R.,
" Commanding Troops."

In this unfortunate affair two officers were killed and two wounded; also 73 non-commissioned officers and men killed and 11 wounded in addition to the naval losses.

Chapter IX.

1855. July. Sabbajee. Nos. 1 & 6 Companies.

In June, 1855, the Sabbajee people began again to give trouble, and early in July, Fodi Osumanu sent a party into British territory to seize a woman whose husband he had already in confinement in Sabbajee.

On the 16th July, Lieut. Davis, 2nd West India Regiment, was sent in command of a small party of the 2nd West India Regiment as an escort to some constables who were ordered to arrest Fodi Osumanu at Sabbajee; he was accompanied by Lieut. Armstrong (3rd West India) and by the Queen's Advocate. On arriving at the town, and after arresting Fodi Osumanu, they were attacked. The prisoner made his escape,

1855. July. Storming of Sabbagee. Nos. 1 & 6 Companies.

and the troops were formed into square and retreated with great steadiness to the fort at Cape St. Mary. The Queen's Advocate narrowly escaped with his life, having been grazed by three bullets ; Lieut. Davis was knocked off his horse, and Lieut. Armstrong had his right arm shattered by a bullet, and subsequently amputated—two men were killed.

On the 17th, the Govenor (Colonel O'Connor, 1st West India Regiment) took with him 120 men of the 1st, 2nd and 3rd West India Regiments, 120 men of the Gambia Militia and 26 enrolled pensioners of the West India Regiments, and proceeded to attack Sabbajee.

The force met with no resistance until they arrived at a wood near to, but through which they had to pass to reach the town. There, a heavy fire was opened by the enemy, which was steadily replied to by the West India troops who were in front, the Militia being kept in reserve—the latter, almost as soon as the firing commenced, retreated in great confusion, notwithstanding the efforts made by their officers to keep them from doing so. The enemy being so numerous, and the jungle they were firing from being so dense, after two hours' fighting it was found necessary to fall back to the fort at Cape St. Mary, distant about 3½ miles

The retreat was carried out steadily, the officers especially behaving with great gallantry, Lieut. Haleman of the 2nd West India Regiment and Lieut. Hill of the 3rd West India Regiment being conspicuous in their efforts to keep back the enemy, who suffered heavy loss. On our side the casualties were very severe.

One officer (Captain Degrigny, who died a

1855. Storming of Sabbajee. Nos. 1 & 6 Companies.

few days after) and 23 men were killed, and two officers (Colonel O'Connor and Staff-Asst.-Surgeon Hendley) and 53 men were wounded.

August 4th.

Assistance was now asked from the French Governor at Goree, who sent all the available seamen and marines he had at his disposal to the assistance of the British. These, to the number of 80 arrived at Bathurst on the 30th of July, and on the 4th of August a force consisting of all the available men of the 1st and 2nd West India, the French contingent and about 600 friendly natives, marched from Cape St. Mary's to attack Sabbajee.

The enemy, as before, made their stand at the wood outside the stockade, defending it most determinately, and it was not until after two hours' hard fighting that the passage through the wood was forced.

The following extract is taken from Ellis's History of the 1st West India:—

" The wood being traversed, the force " debouched upon the plain of Sabbajee, a sandy " level, covered with a scanty growth of guinea " grass and dotted with clumps of dwarf-palms. " The guns were at once placed in position for " breaching the stockade, and fire was opened with " wonderful precision. A few rounds only had " been expended when a large body of natives " from the dis-affected and neighbouring town of " Burnfut made a sudden and determined on- " slaught on our flank, charging furiously forward " with brandished scimetars. This was met " by a party of French marines and the detach- " ments of the 1st and 2nd West India Regiments, " who, after firing a volley at a very close range, " charged gallantly with the bayonet and speedily " routed the enemy, who took refuge in a neigh-

1856. Storming of Sabbajee No. 1 & 6 Companies

"bouring copse. Being ordered to dislodge them "from this cover, the detachments of the 1st and "2nd West India advanced in skirmishing order, "and after a short but sharp conflict, drove them "out on the further side.

" After a bombardment of an hour-and-a-"half, seeing that the enemy extinguished the "thatched roofs of their houses as fast as they were "ignited, and that the ammunition was becoming "exhausted, Lieut.-Colonel O'Connor determined "to carry the stockade by storm. The detach-"ments of the West India Regiments formed up "in the centre, a division of French marines being "on either flank; the whole dashed forward to the "assault in the face of a tremendous fire of "musketry which was opened throughout the "entire length of the loop-holed stockade. In a "few seconds the troops were under the stockade, "which was composed of stout trunks of trees "standing some 18 feet high, and braced on the "inner side by cross-beams. A temporary check "was here experienced (the men having no ladders "for escalading), during which the Mandingoes kept "up a close fire from their upper tier of loop-holes, "while others crouched in the ditch in rear and "cut at the feet and legs of the troops through the "apertures in the stockade on a level with the "ground. The check, however, was of short "duration, for the British opened fire on the "enemy through their own loop-holes, and drove "them back, while others clambering over the "rough defences effected an entrance. The "enemy at once cleared out of the stockade, "many being shot down in their flight. The loss "of the combined force (exclusive of the native "contingent) was 17 killed and 31 wounded."

The following officers of the 2nd West India took part in one or all of these actions, viz.,

1855. Storming of Sabbajee, Nos. 1 & 6 Companies.

Captain Charnack, Lieuts. Davis, Haleman and Joyce.

Colonel O'Connor in his despatch reporting these actions to the home authorities makes the following mention of Lieut. Haleman :—

" I deem it my duty to bring under the " special notice of your Lordship, the conduct of " Lieut. Haleman of the 2nd West India Regi- " ment, who commanded the advanced division on " the line of march composed of detachments of " the 1st and 2nd West India Regiments, and who " gallantly dashed through the wood in the face of " the enemy and afterwards led his party with the " greatest courage and ability through a dense " thicket and routed them."

The following Horse Guards' letter, dated 6th September 1855, was published in General Orders, Gambia, on 26th October.

Horse Guards Letter.

" Sir,

" The General Commander-in-Chief having " had before him the despatches which were " addressed to the Adjutant-General on July 30th " and 6th ultimo, giving an account of the pro- " ceedings from the 16th of July to the 4th of " August last of the force under your command " against the Mahammedan rebel town of " Sabbajee, which was eventually taken by assault " at the point of the bayonet.

" I am directed to assure you of Lord " Hardinge's satisfaction at the perusal of those " despatches, and that he considers the gallantry " and steadiness displayed by the troops on this " occasion, and the judgment with which they " were directed by you to be deserving of high " praise.

1855. "His Lordship further desired that the "expression of his sentiments might be communi- "cated accordingly to yourself and to all the troops "concerned.

"To O.C. Troops, I have, &c., &c.,
" West Africa. (Signed) C. YORK,
" Mil. Secretary."

In these actions the 2nd West India lost:

Losses in Action.

Killed—two Coy.-sergt.-majors and three privates; total five.

Wounded—two corporals and seven privates; total nine.

1855. West Indies. Demerara.

Head-quarters at Demerara were inspected by General W. Wood, C.B., K.H., on the 25th October; at the conclusion, the inspecting officer desired Lieut.-Colonel Whitfeild to make known to the officers, non-commissioned officers and men how much pleased he was with their clean appearance, and steadiness in the ranks, also the precision of their movements on parade.

Regiment Volunteers for Crimea.

"On the 30th August, after a review order "parade," Lieut.-Colonel Whitfeild reports to the General Officer Commanding, "the regiment, "with one accord, expressed their wish to be "allowed to volunteer for the Crimea. . . . . "Having been solicited to make known this loyal "feeling on their behalf to his Excellency the "Lieut.-General commanding, I have only to add "that should they be required, I feel confident this "complete regiment to the number of 1,078 "bayonets will not be found wanting."

To which the following reply was received:

1855. "Horse Guards, 6th November, 1855.
"Sir,
"I have laid before the Field Marshal "Commanding-in-Chief your letter of the 7th "September last, forwarding a copy of a letter "from Lieut.-Colonel Whitfeild, commanding 2nd "West India Regiment, stating that the Corps "wished to be allowed to volunteer for the Crimea "or any other active service, and I am directed by "his Lordship to request that you will thank the "regiment for their good feeling and patriotic "spirit.
"To General Wood, &c., &c.,
" Barbados.
" (Signed) W. F. Forster, D.A.G."

1856. Draft to Africa.

On the 19th January, 1856, a draft consisting of Lieut. Thomson, Ensign Tarte and 85 non-commissioned officers and men embarked at Demerara on board the "*Mary Morton*" to reinforce Nos. 1 and 6 companies on the West Coast of Africa.

Riots in British Guiana.

In February, 1856, a sudden outbreak of serious disturbance occurred at Georgetown and in various parts of the colony of British Guiana. The 2nd West India was called out in aid of civil power. The following extracts of complimentary letters which were received on the occasion are of interest:

No. 1. Extract from Letter from General Officer Commanding to Lieut.-Colonel Whitfeild, dated Barbados, 4th March, 1856.

. . . . . "I have now much satisfaction in "conveying to you His Excellency's unqualified "approbation of all your own proceedings, and of "the conduct of the officers, non-commissioned "officers and soldiers of the 2nd West India "Regiment under your command.

1856. British Guiana.

" The zeal and patient endurance of incessant fatigue, together with forbearance under the " most trying circumstances, and a prompt " obedience to orders as exhibited by all ranks, are " the certain results of a high state of discipline " and efficiency for which the 2nd West India " Regiment is so distinguished and for which it is " so much indebted to your own exertions.

" (Signed) F. D. GEORGE, D.A.G."

No. 2. Letter from the Colonial Office to Military Secretary, Horse Guards, conveying thanks of H.M. Government.

" Downing Street,

Thanks of Her Majesty's Government.

" Sir, 18th April, 1856.

" I am directed by Mr. Secretary Labouchere " to acquaint you that in a despatch which has " been received from the Governor of British " Guiana, reporting serious disturbances which had " occurred there, special mention is made of the " assistance afforded to the authorities by Lieut.- " Colonel Whitfeild, and the officers and men of " the 2nd West India Regiment. I am to enclose " the extract from the minutes of the Court of " Policy on the occasion, and I am to request you " will move the General Commanding-in-Chief, to " cause the thanks of Her Majesty's Government " to be conveyed to Lieut.-Colonel Whitfeild and " the officers and men of his regiment for the " services rendered by them.

" To Major-Gen. York, I have, &c., &c.,

" &c., &c., &c. (Signed) JOHN BALL."

No. 3. Extract from Letter from Military Secretary, Horse Guards, to Lieut.-Colonel Whitfeild.

1856. "In transmitting to you by direction of the "Field Marshal Commanding-in-Chief the accompanying copy of a communication which has "been received from the Colonial Office. . . . . .

" I am desired to express to you the great "satisfaction with which Viscount Hardinge has "perused the minutes of the Court of Policy on "the occasion, especially thanking you and the "officers and men of the 2nd West India Regiment, "for the admirable manner in which a service, "particularly requiring steadiness and good "discipline, was performed.

"To I have, &c., &c.,

" Lt.-Col. Whitfeild. (Signed) C. York."

Thanks of Court of Policy. No. 4. Extract from a Resolution in the Court of Policy, at a special meeting held on the 6th March, 1856.

"Resolved, that the Governor and the "Court of Policy, having, as they earnestly hope, "good reasons for believing that the riots which "have of late prevailed throughout the counties of "Demerara and Essequebo, and partially in that "of Berbice, have now been effectually suppressed, "are anxious to take the earliest opportunity of "expressing the grateful sense which they entertain "of the services of those to whom the colony is "mainly indebted for the restoration of order.

" To Lieut.-Colonel Whitfeild and the "officers and men of the 2nd West India Regiment "their thanks are especially due, for the readiness "and zeal with which their services have been "made available in any shape, and under all "circumstances; the excellent discipline and the "good behaviour of the troops, have excited the

1856. **Riot in British Guiana. Reward to N.C.O.'s & men.**

"admiration of all who had an opportunity of "witnessing their conduct and have entitled them "to the fullest confidence of the Government, and "the community at large. . . . . .

" (Signed) W. WALKER, Sec. Court of Policy."

On the application of Lieut.-Colonel Whitfeild, the undermentioned men were specially granted good conduct medals and gratuities:—

Qr.-Mr.-Sergt. Thos. Mitchell	-	medal and £15.
Sergt. Richard Sheil	- - - -	medal and £9.
Private John Waller	- - - -	medal and £3.
,, John Jones	- - - - -	medal and £3.

These were ordered by Horse Guards' letter, dated June 20th, 1856, and issued to the men on receipt.

Demerara Inspected by Major-General Sir A. Cloete.

On the 17th November, the regiment was inspected by Major-General Sir A. Cloete, and at the conclusion he addressed the regiment to the following effect:—" Lieut.-Colonel Whitfeild, "officers, non-commissioned officers and men of "the 2nd West India, it cannot be more gratifying "to you to receive, than it is for me to give you, "my entire approbation, and to assure you that "everything I have seen of this fine regiment has "given me every satisfaction, not only for your "movements in the field, which have been generally "performed with steadiness and accuracy, but "your system of interior economy, your clean "appearance, the correct manner in which your "books are kept, the neatness of your kits and "messing, and your general behaviour, entitle you "to the highest commendation.

1856. "To you officers, I am happy to inform you "that your Commanding Officer assures me that "he has invariably received from one and all that "cordial support and co-operation so essential to "the well-being of a regiment and which it is "evident, has brought the regiment to such a "state of efficiency that it may well vie with any "in Her Majesty's service, and you may rest "assured that it will give me much pleasure to "report the same in the highest terms to H.R.H. "the General Commanding-in-Chief."

New Accoutrements

In 1856, waist-belts were issued in lieu cross-belt and breast-plate.

Nos. 2 and 4 companies moved from Honduras in December 1856 in H.M.S. "*Perseverance*" to St. Lucia and Barbados respectively, under command of Captain Murray and Lieut. Byrne.

No. 4 company joined head-quarters, Demerara, on the 14th February from Dominica.

1857. Nos. 1 & 6 Companies from Africa to Jamaica.

On the 18th March, Nos. 1 and 6 companies on being relieved by the 1st West India, moved from Africa to Jamaica in H.M.S. "*Perseverance*," landing on 17th April, 1857.

Headquarters from Demerara to Jamaica.

Head-quarters, under command of Lieut.-Colonel Whitfeild, consisting of Nos. 3, 7, 8 and light companies, moved from Demerara on the 4th May, arriving at Jamaica on the 13th May. The following officers were present with head-quarters :

Captains W. E. Mockler and H. W. Steward ;

Lieuts. D. A. Patterson (actg.-pay-mr.) and L. R. Druet (actg. adjt.) ;

1857. Ensigns M. Lynch, E. Oldfield, C. Cradock, W. McCoy, J. Franklin, H. Platt ;

Surgeon J. Mostyn, Asst.-Surgeon T. O'Brien ;

Qr.-Mr. T. Kelly.

No. 3 and light companies disembarked with head-quarters, and Nos. 7 and 8 companies with the undermentioned officers proceeded direct to Belize, but on account of smallpox raging there did not land, but returned to Jamaica and joined head-quarters at Up Park Camp.

Nos. 1 and 6 companies having arrived from Africa in April were stationed at Camp, the following officers being with them, viz., Lieuts. Thomson and Tarte.

No. 2 company joined at the same time from St. Lucia under Captain Murray and Lieut. Wise, and were stationed at Kingston Barracks; but in June, the head-quarters 1st West India moved to Nassau and the 2nd was distributed as follows :—

Distribution of the Regiment, 1857

Nos. 1, 2, 6 and light companies, under Colonel Whitfeild, at Up Park Camp.

No. 3 company at Spanishtown, under Captain Mockler.

Nos. 4 and 5 companies at Demerara, under Captain Ivey.

No. 7 company at Kingston, under Captain Reece.

No. 8 company at Port Royal, under Lieut. R. S. Jones.

1857. The Grenadier company at Trinidad, under Captain Lake.

Jamaica Sword of Honour to Col. Whitfeild.

In May, 1857, the Colony of British Guiana, by a resolution in the Court of Policy, presented Colonel Whitfeild with a sword of honour at the cost of £100—which was voted for that purpose.

Col. S. J. Hill to half-pay & to be Col.-on-Staff at Sierra Leone

Colonel Stephen J. Hill (Senior Lieut.-Colonel of the regiment), who had been Governor and commanding troops at Sierra Leone since 1854, was placed on half-pay in September and appointed Colonel on the Staff—to remain as Governor and in command at Sierra Leone.

Grenadiers to Headquarters.

The Grenadiers, with Nos. 4 and 5 companies, arrived from Trinidad and Demerara on the 4th of July. The Grenadiers, consisting of Captains Lake and Smith, Lieuts. Edwards and Pugh, Asst.-Surgeon Frazer, and 99 non-commissioned officers and men marched to Camp, while Nos. 4 and 5 companies—with Captains Anderson and Ivey, Lieuts. Byrne, King and MacNamara, and 172 non-commissioned officers and men—proceeded in the "*Perseverance*" to Belize.

Dec. 1857. Nos. 4 & 5 Companies to Honduras.

Enfield Rifle Issued.

The regiment received the Enfield rifle (1853 pattern) in June, 1857.

Establishment 1295 N.C.O.'s and men.

On the 31st of October, 1857, orders were received to raise the establishment to 1,295 non-commissioned officers and men, which was accomplished by the end of the year by recruiting parties sent out through Jamaica, Antigua and Barbados.

The regiment was inspected by Major-General Bell on the 19th November, 1857, and His Royal Highness's remarks on the Inspection

1858. Report were as follows:—"The state of the 2nd "West India Regiment is very satisfactory to His "Royal Highness."

Jamaica. No. 9 Company to Honduras.

On the 29th of March, No. 9 company, with Lieut.-Colonel Gibbons, Captain Scott, Lieuts. Edwards and McCoy, Ensigns DeLancy, Knapp, Russell, Lewis, and Assistant.-Surgeon O'Brien, and 159 non-commissioned officers and men embarked on H.M.S. "*Leopard*" for Honduras.

In this year (1858), the Regiment was reduced to the ordinary establishment.

Zouave Uniform.

Zouave uniform was issued to the Regiment towards the end of 1858.

Chapter X.

Jamaica.
1859.
In aid of
Civil Power.

In March, 1859, serious disturbances took place in the parish of Westmoreland, and the regiment was employed in establishing order, which was not finally done till October of that year.

1860.
Inspection by
Maj.-Gen.
Taylor.

In June, 1860, the Regiment was inspected by Major-General Taylor, and the following flattering letter was received from the Adjutant-General :—

" Horse Guards, 2nd August, 1860.
" Sir,
" By direction of the General Commanding-
" in-Chief, I have the honour to acknowledge
" the receipt of your confidential report of the 2nd
" West India Regiment, which His Royal Highness
" deems most satisfactory.

1860. " The Duke of Cambridge has expressed "himself in terms of high commendation of this "excellent regiment and its able Commanding "Officer Colonel Whitfeild.

" (Signed) J. YORK SCARLETT, A.G.

Six Companies to Africa.

It having been directed by the home authorities (by Horse-guards' letter dated 2nd January, 1856,) that the three West India Regiments were in future to furnish six companies in succession for duty on the west coast, the remaining four companies in the West Indies to act as a "Depôt to receive and train recruits and "maintain the efficiency of the companies on the "coast of Africa."

The 2nd West India was in 1860 ordered to furnish a wing consisting of six companies to relieve the wing of the 1st West India, which had been in Africa since 1857.

H.M.S. "*Perseverance*," having embarked three companies (4, 5 and 9) at Belize, proceeded to Jamaica, embarking three companies (Nos. 6, 7 and 8) on the 23rd September—the whole under command of Major T. H. Smith. The following officers accompanied the wing:—Captains Mockler, Jones, Willcocks and Byrne, Lieuts. Forbes, Eyre, Russell, Brett and MacNamara, Ensigns Lowry, Bowers, Madden, Drinan and Coward, Staff-Asst.-Surgeon MacAuly, 588 non-commissioned officers and men, besides the usual number of women and children.

Wreck of the 'Perseverance' October 21st, 1860

On the 21st of October, having passed St. Vincent on the 20th, the "*Perseverance*" struck on a reef three-quarters of a mile from the Island of Maio; she was under full steam at the time, and filled so rapidly that officers and men had to abandon their clothes, arms, and accoutrements and make for the Island of Maio in the ship's boats.

1860. Four companies, with seven officers, were forwarded in the barque "*King Fisher*" to Gambia.

Arrival at Sierra Leone.

H.M.S. "*Espoir*" conveyed one officer and 71 non-commissioned officers and men, and H.M.S. "*Industry*" conveyed five officers and 145 non-commissioned officers and men, besides 15 women and 23 children to Sierra Leone. The "*Espoir*" arriving at Sierra Leone on the 16th and the "*Industry*" on the 20th of November, 1860.

On the 11th of November, ss. "*Armenian*" arrived at Sierra Leone from the Gambia with one officer, 104 non-commissioned officers and men, six women, and six children. This made a distribution of three companies at Gambia and three companies at Sierra Leone.

Every article of kit was lost in the wreck, officers, men, women and children had nothing except what they stood in.

Lieut.-Colonel Murray (1st West India Regiment), who was in command at Sierra Leone, directed the issue of a shirt, white trousers and a fatigue jacket of an obsolete pattern to each man—the men, on landing, having nothing but their sea check shirts and trousers.

Captain Byrne and Lieut. MacNamara died on the passage from the West Indies, the former on the 23rd and the latter on the 25th of September from fever.

Major W. Hill, having previously arrived from England, assumed command of the detachment at Sierra Leone.

1860. Arrival at Sierra Leone. Although the War Office allowed some compensation for losses, still in many instances it was wholly inadequate. For instance, nothing was allowed for the kits of women and children, as there was "No provisions in the regulation authorising it." £50 only was allowed for mess kit, and wine, although the value of the wine lost amounted to over £250 alone.

1861. Baddiboo War. On the arrival of the companies at the Gambia in October, 1860, they found that a blockade of the kingdom of Baddiboo had been commenced, and that the gunners of the 1st West India were employed on this duty. On December 11th, all the gunners present of the 2nd West India Regiment were sent up to relieve the gunners of the 1st West India.

The transport "*Avon*," which had been despatched from England to convey the 1st West India to the West Indies, in consequence of the loss of the "*Perseverance*," arrived on the 12th of January, 1861. Colonel D'Arcy determined, if he could get sufficient force at his command, to make an example of the king; he accordingly went in the "*Avon*" to Sierra Leone, and there embarked three companies of the 1st West India and one of the 2nd and returned to the Gambia with this additional force, arriving at Bathurst on the 2nd of February.

The expeditionary force now consisted of six companies of the 1st West India (under command of Lieut.-Colonel Murray), and four companies of the 2nd West India (under command of Major W. Hill), Colonel D'Arcy, the Governor, being present, but not in active command.

On the 15th of February, six companies embarked upon H.M. *ss.* "*Torch*," "*Avon*," colonial

1861. Baddiboo War.

steamer "*Dover*" and schooners "*Elizabeth*" and "*Margaret*," and proceeded up the river to Swarra Cunda Creek about 40 miles from Bathurst. The "*Dover*," after distributing the two companies she had on board amongst the three other vessels, returned to Bathurst and brought up two companies of the 1st and two of the 2nd West India besides the Gambia Militia, of which the Governor was honorary Colonel, also Captain Lamorciere and 12 European gunners from the settlement of Goree.

On the following morning (16th February) the expedition moved down a creek which separates the kingdoms of Barra and Baddiboo to a landing place about 20 miles from the king's town of Indear, which had been reconnoitred previously by Major Hill; this landing-place was found to be covered by a strong earthwork, loop-holed and well manned.

The "*Torch*," with as many troops as she could take on board, anchored about 180 yards from the earthwork, and the natives were warned that if they did not surrender, the guns of the "*Torch*" would open fire in half-an-hour—they replied with yells of defiance.

1861. Baddiboo Expedition, February.

After the lapse of half-an-hour the guns of the "*Torch*," opened fire, while the troops poured in a heavy musketry fire; when this had lasted over two hours, the natives began to abandon their works and arrangements were made to land; it was then found that no means had been provided for manning the boats, and the complement of European sailors being but small, it was decided to postpone the landing until next morning.

At this decision great dissatisfaction was felt and the officers 2nd West India volunteered to

1861. Baddiboo Expedition. February.

row the boats ashore ; on this being acceded to arrangements were again made to land.

As the boats rounded the bow of the "*Torch*" the enemy were seen leaving their position. Lieut. Walsh, 2nd West India, was the first to land closely followed by Pte. Nisbett, who saved Lieut. Walsh's life by bayonetting a native as he was in the act of shooting him.

Before a landing could be effected some 800 natives, who had occupied the extreme right of the earthwork which had not suffered from our fire, rushed down to oppose the landing, however, the troops attacked them with the bayonet, which soon scattered them in all directions. Colonel D'Arcy in his despatch says :—

" Nothing could exceed the gallantry of the " landing on the part of the officers and men of the " 1st and 2nd West India Regiments, and now " commenced a smart skirmish with a numerous " enemy in which our black soldiers evinced a " gallantry and determination to close, which I felt " proud to witness."

The following is an extract of Ellis's History of the 1st West India Regiment :—

" While this stubborn and hand to hand " conflict was at its height, a shrill cry was " suddenly heard in rear of the enemy, and at " once, as if by a preconcerted plan, those natives " who were disputing the landing broke and fled, " while at the same time a body of some 300 " cavalry debouched from the shelter of a clump " of dwarf paling and came down at full gallop on " the troops who already were somewhat scattered " in pursuit of the retreating enemy. The men at " once formed rallying squares, and in a moment " the Mandingo horsemen were amongst them,

1861. Baddiboo Expedition. "brandishing their scimitars and discharging "matchlocks and pistols; the fire from the squares "was so well sustained that with one exception "the enemy could effect nothing.

"They rode round and round the squares "for a few minutes uttering shouts of defiance and "endeavouring to reach the men with their spears; "and finally, a good many saddles having been "emptied, galloped off as rapidly as they had "come; their long robes streaming out behind in "the wind.

"The one exception referred to, was a group "of three men of the 1st and two of the 2nd "West India, who, having advanced too far in "pursuit, had become separated from their "comrades, and on the sudden appearance of the "cavalry, had not time to reach any of the squares, "they stood back to back surrounded by the enemy, "until they were overwhelmed by force of numbers, "and ridden down, being afterwards found lying "where they had stood surrounded by eleven dead "Mandingoes whom they had shot or bayonetted."

February. This finished the fight and the troops bivouacked on the ground for the night.

On the 17th the Gambia Militia (Artillery) arrived and landed, and the same afternoon the 1st and 2nd West India Regiments, after a short resistance, took and destroyed the stockaded town of Carawan.

At 9 o'clock the next morning, 18th February, H.M.S. "*Arrogant*" arrived with Commodore Edmonstone: a party of sailors and marines were landed, and about noon the force marched on the sacred Mandingo town of Sabba, burning the town of Kinty Cunda *en route*. Sabba was

1861. Baddiboo Expedition.

attacked and burnt, and the troops returned to their camp.

It was then determined to attack the King's town—Indear, and the 19th and 20th were passed in the necessary preparations, but in the afternoon an escaped slave girl, brought intelligence that a strong force of the King's warriors had come from Indear and were stockading Sabba.

Storming of Sabba.

The troops returned over the same ground and found the town defended by a double stockade and well manned.

The troops were formed for attack, the 1st West India (4 companies) on the right, seamen and marines in the centre, the 2nd West India (4 companies) on the left, while the reserve consisted of two companies 1st West India.

The Howitzer Battery, commanded by Captain R. S. W. Jones, 2nd West India, which was between the centre and left divisions, opened fire; the enemy attacked both flanks, advancing through the high grass and bush; a hot fire was kept up for some little time and finally the centre division, seamen and marines, were thrown out in skirmishing order and dashed at the stockade, attacking the enemy with the bayonet, drove them out with the loss of one officer, Lieut. Hamilton of the "*Arrogant*" and three men killed, and twenty-two wounded.

The flanking divisions acting in concert advanced, and completed the rout.

The total loss in this engagement was, killed, one officer and three men. Wounded, one officer and forty-four men.

1861. **Baddiboo Expedition.** After the destruction of Sabba, the enemy sued for peace, which they obtained by paying a heavy fine, and by making restitution to the traders, who had been plundered.

The six companies of the 1st West India embarked for the West Indies on the 3rd March, the company of the 2nd belonging to the Sierra Leone Garrison arriving there on the 11th March in H.M.S. "*Falcon.*" Major Hill also returned to Sierra Leone in H.M.S. "*Arrogant,*" arriving there on the 9th March.

The following were the 13 officers 2nd West India Regiment engaged in the Baddiboo Expedition.

Major W. Hill; Captains—R. S. Jones, Mockler, Willcocks; Lieuts.—Platt, Walsh, Russell and Eyre; Ensigns—Bowers, Lowry, Madden, Drinan and Coward.

Abbeokuta. In March 1861 on the return of the troops from the Gambia, an application was made by the British Consul at Lagos for assistance in the defence of the town of Abbeokuta against an expected attack from the King of Dahomy. A detachment 2nd West India, consisting of 6 officers, 260 non-commissioned officers and men under command of Captain R. S. Jones were ordered to proceed there in H.M.S. "*Arrogant.*" After a portion of this force had been embarked Commodore Edmonstone considered that the season was too advanced to undertake an expedition, and consequently the troops were disembarked and the order cancelled.

Instead of this, Captain A. T. Jones, one sergeant and eleven rank and file were dispatched in the "*Arrogant*" to Abbeokuta to instruct the Egbas in gunnery and assist in placing the town

1861. Abbeokuta. in a proper state of defence; they sailed from Sierra Leone on the 24th March, the N.C.O. and men returned to Sierra Leone on the 19th July, but Captain Jones unfortunately died at Abbeokuta on the 7th July.

March, 1861. Quiah. Early in March of this year the war men of the Quiah country invaded the British island of Tombo, maltreated a resident merchant, plundering his stores, and when Captain R. S. Jones, 2nd West India Regiment at the request of the Governor, with the Inspector of Police proceeded up the river to demand redress for the outrage committed on the person of a British subject, and the insult offered to our flag, the natives exhibited the greatest violence, threatening to take the lives of both these officers. On their return to Freetown on the 18th, it was decided at once to dispatch an expedition into the Quiah country, and on the 19th a force of 3 officers and 130 non-commissioned officers and men under command of Captain R. S. Jones was depatched to Waterloo, a town on the frontier, about 30 miles distant from Freetown, to defend it in case of attack, while a force of 5 officers and 167 non-commissioned officers and men were ordered to embark at 2 p.m. on the 20th to proceed up the Sierra Leone River in boats in company with a force of seamen and marines of the "*Arrogant*" and "*Falcon*." However at 1 p.m. Bey Cantah, the King of the Quiah country, arrived at Freetown, and gave himself up to the Governor, and promised that his war men by whom the acts of aggression had been committed, should be handed over to the British Government, whereupon the order for embarkation was cancelled, for the present, and the detachment at Waterloo reduced to one sergeant and twelve men.

1861. May. Quiah War. On the 15th May, reports came to the Governor that the Quiah people had expressed their determination to attack and burn Waterloo and Campbelltown, in consequence of which a detachment, under command of Lieut. Russell, was sent to garrison those towns, 47 extra n.c.o's. and men to Waterloo, and 40 to Campbelltown, which places were only four miles apart; this had a quieting effect, and Bey Cantah agreed to give over to the British that territory of which he was nominally king; but the people he had not the power to keep in restraint.

July. In July it was not considered necessary to keep such a strong force on detached duty, and the reinforcements which had been sent out in May were withdrawn.

November. The Quiah people were dissatisfied and restless, not liking the action of their King in yielding to the British, and as soon as the troops were removed, they recommenced assembling their war parties, and were a menace to the native settlers, who were afraid to remain on their farms as long as these parties were roving about.

In consequence of this it was considered advisable in order to re-establish confidence, to again garrison Waterloo with a strong company.

This was accordingly done, and on the 22nd November, Captain R. S. Jones, Lieut. E. Forbes, Asst.-Surgeon Oakes, and 126 non-commissioned officers and men marched to Waterloo, and from there to Madonkia.

At this time no actual hostilities were expected, but as later events showed, troops had not been sent out before they were required.

1861. Quiah War.

On the 26th November, reports came into Madonkia that the Timmanies had attacked the Songo people in British Quiah, and the same evening Cabannah Burroh arrived with some of his war men to ask for assistance. At four o'clock next morning, Captain Jones marched a force consisting of Lieut. Forbes, Asst.-Surgeon Oakes, 95 non-commissioned officers and men, and one rocket tube to Songotown, arriving there a little after seven o'clock. After resting and having breakfast, the detachment marched in conjunction with Cabannah Burroh and his war men, at about 10 o'clock to follow up the enemy. At about 12 o'clock they came on their track and followed them closely for about two hours or rather more, until they arrived at Kabaie on the bank of the river Ribbee, a distance of about 25 miles. The river was about 120 yards wide at that place.

Kabaie, November 27th

The enemy were seen lining the banks on the opposite side, but as the river was very deep, and there were no boats, the troops were unable to follow them up. The Timmanies began firing as soon as the troops appeared, but without doing any damage; a few volleys from the Enfield rifles, and some rockets soon drove the enemy from the bank.

After resting for half-an-hour the troops started on their return, Lieut. Forbes in command of the rear-guard; they had not marched more than 400 yards when the Timmanies commenced to attack them in rear. The column was halted, and Captain Jones reinforced the rear-guard. After a few minutes' heavy firing, the enemy disappeared, but before doing so some of them actually came into the open uttering their war cries, and brandishing their weapons. The casualties in this affair were, 2nd West India Regiment—killed—Lc.-Corporal E. Smith, No. 9 company, and a few

1861. Quiah War. November 27th

slightly wounded—including Lieut. Forbes; war men, six wounded.

Amongst the enemy the casualties were very severe, 30 being killed and many wounded.

Captain Jones, considering it imprudent to remain for the night in such dense and swampy locality, determined to push on to Madonkia, where he arrived with his detachment at 11.30 p.m., having marched 40 miles since 4 a.m. that morning,in a country, the roads being nothing more than dried watercourses, through dense jungle, high grass, and swamp, in some places so deep, that logs had to be laid down before the troops could pass over, the men having to march the whole way in Indian file.

In concluding his official report, Captain R. S. Jones states: " The men behaved extremely " well, and I received every assistance from Lieut. " Forbes and Dr. Oakes. Both behaved with great " coolness in the presence of the enemy. Lieut. " Forbes was slightly grazed on the hip with a " slug."

Next morning, Captain Jones marched his detachment from Madonkia, leaving at six o'clock and arriving at Waterloo at nine o'clock, having received orders to do so.

As soon as the news reached Freetown, the governor, Colonel S. Hill, requested Major Hill to move all available troops into Quiah country, and embodied three companies of the Sierra Leone Militia.

On the 2nd December, the following detail left Freetown for Waterloo: — Major Hill, Captain A. Williams, Lieuts. Russell (garri-

1861. Quiah War. November 27th son adjutant) and Brett, 2nd West India Regiment; Staff-Asst.-Surgeon Morphew, D.A.C.G. Hunter, and D.A.S. of Works Relph.

The Timmanies by this time had established themselves in force at a town called Massago, situated on the north bank of the Waterloo creek, and had endeavoured to intercept the traffic of the river by firing on the boats, some of which they had succeeded in capturing.

At 10 p.m., on the 7th December, Major Hill embarked a party in canoes consisting of two officers and 117 n.c.o's. and men, in order to make a night attack on Massago; on arriving near the town the natives who were working the canoes got frightened and could not be induced to proceed, and as the attack was meant to be a surprise, it was considered that the object would be defeated owing to this difficulty with the canoe hands. Major Hill decided to defer the attack, and returned to Waterloo.

On Tuesday, 10th December, the same party started at 9 a.m., in boats rowed by seamen from H.M.S. "*Torch*" and "*Falcon*," and landed under cover of light guns fired from the ships' pinnaces. They found that the enemy had cleared out as soon as the firing commenced, leaving everything behind them, even food cooking on the fires; after thoroughly destroying the town, the troops returned to Waterloo.

The road from Waterloo to Songo (or Prince Alfred's) town, being practically unfit for use, a large gang of natives, protected by a covering party of one officer and 100 men, were employed daily, in making a new road. This duty was undertaken alternately by Royal Sierra Leone Militia and the 2nd West India Regiment.

1861. Quiah War.

Later on this party was increased to two officers and 150 men, and was furnished principally by the 2nd West India Regiment.

On the 3rd December, a small detachment of 50 men, under command of Lieut. Brett, was sent forward to Songotown; he was attacked on the way, but not seriously inconvenienced, except that his carriers halted on the first shot being fired, and this caused considerable delay.

Chapter XI.

1861.
Storming of Madonkia 19th December

On the 18th December information was received at Waterloo that the Timmanies had made a large stockade at Madonkia, and that Cabannah Burroh had attacked them, but was defeated.

Major Hill immediately sent a messenger to Songotown to tell Cabannah Burroh to meet him with his war men at Madonkia at 10 a.m. next day, 19th; he also sent a similar message to the Kosso chief at Cacoetown.

The following morning, at eight o'clock, a force, under command of Major Hill, started for Madonkia, consisting of Captains R. S. Jones and Williams, 130 n.c.o's. and men 2nd West India, and 22 n.c.o's. and men of the Royal Sierra Leone Militia, Staff-Asst.-Surgeon Morphew and

1861. Quiah War. Storming of Madonkia. 19th December.

D.A.C.G. Thompson, one howitzer and two rocket tubes. On the way the Kosso war men joined them, but Cabannah Burroh did not put in an appearance.

The force marched direct on Madonkia, arriving at the creek at about three p.m.; here it was found necessary to make a bridge for the troops to pass over. Skirmishers were thrown out to prevent the working party being molested.

As soon as the bridge was ready the troops moved over, and the howitzer and rocket tubes were at once brought into action; the men were formed into a semi-circle, lying down under cover, the guns being in the centre. The shelling was most successfully carried out, all, with the exception of one, bursting inside the stockade.

The following description from the official report will shew the strength of the work:

"Outside the stockade and about six feet "from it was a war fence, which had to be got "through before the stockade was reached; this "fence was made of poles, about four inches in "diameter, and about 16 or 18 feet high, let in to the "ground about three feet, and bound together with "country rope in three different places.

"The stockade was made of strong beams of "wood, and trees about one foot in diameter, crossed "obliquely with the same and loopholed. There "was also a small tower built in the front on the "stockade, about 20 feet high, big enough for two "or three men to sit in."

After the firing had been continued for a few minutes, the enemy began moving out in small parties; these were shot down by the troops as

1861. Quiah War, Storming of Madonkia. they came out. At this time Major Hill was wounded by a ball in the shoulder, and had to be moved to the rear. Captain R. S. Jones assuming command, decided to storm the work at once, and divided the troops into three parties ; the right party being commanded by Captain Williams, the centre by Captain R. S. Jones, and the left by a sergeant.

They went forward at a rush, but were several minutes before they could break through the war fence. This done, they attacked and broke through the stockade. As soon as the fence was broken through, the enemy precipitately retreated into the town in rear, a party of Kossos were sent after them, and they dispersed them thoroughly. The front and sides of the stockade were then pulled down, and the whole place burnt. The force then returned to Waterloo, which they reached at 11.30 p.m., leaving a party of Kossos to occupy Madonkia.

In front of the stockade was found the heads of three Kosso prisoners (whom they had taken two days previously), being dried in the smoke of a small fire.

Captain Jones, in reporting this affair, finished by stating:—" With regard to the N.C.O's. " and men, I have much pleasure in stating their " behaviour in presence of the enemy was every- " thing that I could desire."

The following were the casualties—2nd West India Regiment—in this action :

Major Hill wounded dangerously ;

Captains Jones and Williams wounded slightly ;

1861. Quiah War.

One sergeant killed, one wounded ;

Three privates wounded dangerously—total, eight.

Major Hill was conveyed to Freetown for treatment, leaving Captain Jones in command at Waterloo.

Defence of Songotown.

On the 21st December, Songo, or Prince Alfred's-town, was attacked by a strong force of Timmanies. The enemy, unperceived by the watchmen of the irregular troops, succeeded in getting quite close to the town, and forced a small stockade, which was occupied by them for the purpose of guarding one of the principal approaches ; having done this, they, headed by one of their chiefs, advanced almost into the town. Lieut. Brett, having got his detachment under arms, poured in a close and well-directed fire, which, aided by rockets fired at a short distance, caused much confusion amongst the enemy.

The attack lasted about two hours and was well sustained, after which, the enemy having suffered severely, retired.

Lieut. Brett, as soon as he was attacked, despached a message to Waterloo, reporting he was hard pressed, and asking for assistance.

The enemy were over three hundred strong; their killed and wounded were reported as being 150,which shews how determinately they advanced to the attack. A number of bodies were found afterwards, although it was the invariable custom of the natives to carry away their dead to avoid their being mutilated.

The casualties on our side were five men wounded.

1861. Quiah War. Defence of Songotown. December 21st.

In reporting this affair to the Adjutant-General, Major Hill states as follows :—

"I am glad to state that Lieut. Brett and "the 50 men of his detachment succeeded, after a "sharp contest with a few wounded on our side, "in repulsing the enemy, whose loss, I have heard "since, is very considerable.

" I would bring under the notice of the "General Commanding-in-Chief, the gallant "conduct of Lieut. Brett and the small detach-"ment of the 2nd West India Regiment under his "command, and I trust that H.R.H. will be pleased "with the conduct exhibited by the troops on this "occasion."—Dated Sierra Leone, 15th January, 1862.

On the 26th December, information was received that the enemy had established themselves at Robea, and a force, under command of Captain R. S. Jones, was ordered to proceed there at 10 a.m. on the 27th. That officer's report is so interesting that I give it in full; it is dated Waterloo, 29th December, 1861.

Re-taking of Madonkia.

Report—"In obedience to your instructions, "I prepared to march on Robea, but at about 1.30 "on that day I received intelligence that the "Kossos had been attacked and driven out of "Madonkia; I therefore marched at 2.30 to their "relief. My force consisted of Captain Williams, "Lieut. Russell and 160 men of the 2nd West "India Regiment, with Captain Jolly and Lieut. "Beckles and 50 men of the Sierra Leone Militia, "one commissariat officer, and one officer of the "military store department, two 12-pr. howitzers, "two rocket tubes, and two days' provisions, "which were carried by 200 carriers.

1861. Quiah War. Re-taking of Madonkia.

" We arrived at Madonkia Creek at about 7 " p.m., when Lieut. Russell, who commanded the " advanced guard, threw them out in skirmishing " order on the edge of the creek, and then made a " bridge of poles for the passage of the troops; the " bridge made by your instructions on the 18th " instant had been destroyed by the enemy.

" On the arrival of the main body the " advance moved forward, and, coming to the place " where the water again crosses the road, (about " the spot where during the former engagement at " Madonkia, he was fired into by the enemy), they, " having cleared away the bush on the left-hand " side, and built another stockade, but without " a war fence round it, immediately pushed " forward and took the place before the enemy " were prepared to defend it. The main body " going forward at the same time, the enemy were " totally routed.

" I then had all pulled down, and burnt; " having placed my stores, ammunition, &c., in " the centre of the ground where the former " stockade was, and thrown out my picquets, I " placed my two guns and rocket tubes in position, " commanding the two roads. Fire having been " lit on account of the darkness, we bivouacked " for the night. I am glad to say the casualties " were only two wounded, the first in the stockade " —Privates Nesbitt and Nicholas.

" The moon rising about 2 a.m. on the 28th, " I sent the two wounded men into Waterloo with " an escort. I then had every piece of wood " burnt that could be found, and at 4 a.m. marched " for Massan Key where I heard the enemy were, " but on our arrival found they had evacuated the " place: so, without delay, I pushed forward to " Mafilla, a large town, where I found a great " preparation for stockading.

1861. Quiah War.

" I halted there about 10 minutes, during "which time I received your communication, " dated 27th instant.

Robea. December 28th

" About 7.30 I marched on Robea; on the " advanced guard reaching the town, they found " the road strongly stockaded across, and heard " the people inside pounding their rice. The " troops crept quietly up to within 50 yards when " they were apparently perceived, a cry being " raised and several horns blown, and a heavy fire " opened upon them; but, being provided with " rockets, Lieut. Russell had them fired into the " town, one of which set fire to the thatch of a " house, causing great consternation among the " enemy, and before they had time to man the " stockade sufficiently he carried it by storm, and " entered the town; Staff-Assistant-Surgeon Gore, " who was with the advance, being the first in.

" On hearing the first shot, I pressed forward " after the advanced guard. The town was soon " enveloped in flames, and the enemy driven from " it into the jungle, with which it is densely sur- " rounded.

" The only buildings which were left " unconsumed were a large one, very high, and a " smaller one beside it, with a grave inside: over " the grave a quantity of liquid had been poured, " and there were a number of 'gregories,' with " three padlocks, and other rubbish.

" This appears to have been one of their " Fetish houses which I burnt and totally destroyed " before leaving it.

" It was now about 10 o'clock, and after " breakfast (a little after 11) we were fired into

1861. Quiah War. Taking of Robea.

" from several directions from the surrounding " thickets. My men immediately returned it in " heavy volleys and the enemy were, for a time, " silenced; but in a quarter-of-an-hour they again " fired into us, when I returned it with the "Howitzers and rockets with the cost of one man " killed and two wounded.

" Having a long march before me, and the sun " being excessively hot, and the officers and men " muchfatigued, I deemed it expedient to return to " Madonkia before dark, especially as I expected " Mafilla would be partially stockaded on my " return, I therefore wished by day-light to see my " way through it.

" Having given the necessary instructions, " the advanced guard moved forward; they had " not proceeded more than half-a-mile when they " were fired into from the jungle, which was " quickly returned and the enemy again quieted. " I left a rocket tube in charge of Dep.-Asst.- " Sup. of Stores Relph, who kindly volunteered " his services with the rear guard; who, when they " got a few 100 yards from the town were also fired " upon from the jungle; they immediately faced " about and fired a few volleys into the bush also " two or three rockets. They remained there " some time, but as there was no further annoy- " ance from the enemy they moved on.

" When I arrived at Mafilla I found all " quiet, and directed the poles and wood gathered " there for stockading to be gathered and burnt, " which was done.

" At this time two of my officers were seen " struck, Staff.-Asst.-Surgeon Morphew and Lieut. " Beckles (Royal Sierra Leone Militia). Having " procured stretchers I marched to Madonkia

1861. Quiah War. Taking of Robea. 28th December "where I intended to remain during the night, but "as Dr. Gore was anxious to have the sick and "wounded conveyed to Waterloo, it being about "4 o'clock, after the men had received half a gill "of grog each I marched direct to Waterloo, "where I arrived about 8.30 p.m.

"The casualties in this action were four "wounded in the 2nd West India Regiment; the "Militia and Kossos lost one killed and 12 "wounded.

"The distance marched in the two days "was not short of 50 miles, besides the work of "destruction of building, &c., and fighting."

In reporting this affair to the Adjutant-General, Major Hill concluded by remarking:—

"I would particularly remark on the energy "and skill that has been displayed by Captain "Jones on every occasion since the commence-"ment of this war; and, had I not been wounded, "I would before this have brought to your notice "the gallant conduct exhibited by this officer, in "the capture after an obstinate resistance of the "enemy's stockade at Madonkia.

" (Signed) W. HILL, MAJOR.

"Dated 15th January, 1862."

1862. On the 15th January, 1862, Major Hill wrote home urgently recommending that more troops should be stationed at Sierra Leone, pointing out that the war had now lasted two months and might continue some time, as his small force—280 all ranks—did not admit of any extensive operations, and that the inhabitants of the frontier towns were such cowards that no reliance could be placed on them. He goes on to say that he had

1862. Quiah War. 300 Militia serving with his men, but that they were so undisciplined that he did not consider them equal to 100 of the 2nd West India.

On the 11th January, Ensign G. Coward joined from the Gambia.

Information having been received on the 10th January at Freetown that the enemy had erected stockades at a factory belonging to Mr. Jolly on the Ribbee River, about 30 miles from the sea, it was determined to dislodge them.

Major Hill directed Captain Jones to come into Freetown with a detachment consisting of Lieut. Russell and 105 non-commissioned officers and men 2nd West India, and one captain and 21 men Royal Sierra Leone Militia. This force arrived in the "*Dover*," at Freetown, on the 14th January, and was there joined by Major Hill, who was still unfit for active work and only able to advise; also by Captain Heneage, three officers and 46 seamen of H.M.S. "*Falcon*," and three boats with guns on board, the naval force being intended to cover the landing of the troops. The "*Dover*" started for the Ribbee on the morning of the 15th, arriving at the mouth of that river at 6 p.m.—there they stopped for the night.

Ribbee Expedition. January 16-18. Next morning (16th), the "*Dover*" proceeded up the river, arriving at Mr. Jolly's factory at 2 p.m., and, as everything was quiet and the natives had not made a stockade, it was not considered advisable to interfere with them.

The force then proceeded to Mr. Headle's factory, 10 miles further up the river, and there ascertained that about four miles further up the river there were two fortified towns called Majembah and Majohn, belonging to Labai

1862. Quiah War. Taking of Majembah.

Bundoo, a chief who had been hostile ; these it was decided to destroy.

At 6 a.m. next morning (17th), the troops under command of Captain Jones proceeded up the river in boats, accompanied by the three "*Falcon*" boats and Captain Heneage's Gig. At 7.30 the force took up a position opposite Majembah, situated at a turn in the river, which is about 50 or 60 yards wide with a reach of about half-a-mile on each side of the town. The boats containing the troops stopped immediately opposite the town. The "*Falcon*" boats being placed on the flanks, at once opened fire with shell, case, and rockets, making some excellent practice.

The troops after a little while landed without opposition, the enemy having been driven out of the town by the shelling. They thoroughly destroyed the town, after which they embarked with the intention of proceeding to and of destroying Majohn.

They had no sooner started than a heavy fire was poured upon the boats from both sides of the river ; this was replied to by both soldiers and sailors, the latter using case shot, which was very effective. Nothing could be seen of the enemy, as the bush on each side was very dense, but the smoke from their guns gave sufficient indication of their whereabouts.

Taking of Majohn. 17th January.

On arrival at Majohn, about 9 a.m., the boats were again fired upon from both sides of the river. The boats took up the same position as before, and after the town had been shelled, together with the surrounding bush and a house set on fire by the rockets, the troops landed ; and having taken proper precautions to prevent surprise, totally destroyed the town, after which

1862. **Quiah War. Taking of Majohn.**

they embarked and pulled to the "*Dover*," arriving on board about 10 a.m.

In reporting this affair to the Adjt.-General, Major Hill, in his letter of 20th January, 1862, particularly mentioned Lieut. Russell for his gallant conduct. Also "Captain Jones exhibited "his usual gallant conduct and good judgment in "carrying out the orders he had received."

The casualties in this expedition were killed, two seamen; wounded, Captain Heneage, and seven seamen, H.M.S. "*Falcon*"; of the 2nd West India, 5 men wounded, one boatman killed and one wounded. Total killed and wounded—17.

Conclusion of War.

The force returned to Freetown on the same day, Captain Jones and his party at once proceeding to Waterloo.

Orders were received on the 18th from the Governor to cease from active operations, as the chiefs and head men had sent in to sue for peace, which was concluded on the 1st February at Freetown.

The following complimentary letter, dated 3rd February, was addressed to Major Hill by Colonel S. Hill, the Governor of Sierra Leone:—

"Sir,

"I have the honour to request that you will "accept for yourself and convey to the officers, "non-commissioned officers and privates, as well "as the officers of the military staff under your "command, my high appreciation of the services "rendered to this colony by their courage and "endurance during the late war in Quiah, which "has been brought to a satisfactory conclusion by

1862. Quiah War. Conclusion. "their distinguished conduct and contempt of "danger and difficulties under very trying "circumstances.

"It will be my pleasing duty to bring under "the notice of Her Majesty's principal Secretary "of State for the colonies, the faithful and dis-"tinguished services rendered by yourself and "those under your command to the colony under "my charge."

On the 24th January, 200 of the Sierra Leone Militia were escourted into Freetown (after having been disarmed) by a detachment 2nd West India Regiment, and there disbanded in disgrace for mutinous conduct.

On the 11th February, two companies returned to Freetown from Waterloo, leaving one company temporally there.

For the above services Major Hill and Captain Jones received Brevet promotion.

1860. West Indies. The following moves in the meantime had taken place in the West Indies :—

On the 7th November, 1860, a detachment of 66 non-commissioned officers and men under command of Major Mends embarked for Honduras.

1861. Headquarters moved to Belize. On the 23rd April, 1861, in consequence of disturbances at Belize, the head-quarters and four companies moved there from Jamaica with the following officers, viz., Col. Whitfeild, Captains Reece, Drouet, Wise, Knapp ; Lieuts. Turton and Matthews ; Ensign Ross ; Assist.-Surgeons Davidge and Wales ; and 295 non-commissioned officers and men.

1861. Head-quarters moved to Belize.

On the departure of the head-quarters, the inhabitants of Jamaica presented a most flattering address, which goes on to say :—

" We hope it will not be considered in- " trusive if we say that the regiment under your " command is, and has been in such a state of " discipline, as to elicit the admiration of all, " whether professional or non-professional. . . . "

Head-quarters moved to Nassau.

On the 15th May. the head-quarters embarked at Belize on board transport "*Avon*," and proceeded to Nassau, arriving there on the 21st.

Nassau. New Colours. presented by Prince Alfred.

On the 4th December, 1862, new colours were presented to the regiment by Prince Alfred, who, at the conclusion, addressed the regiment as follows :—" I have very great pleasure in present- " ing these colours to the 2nd West India " Regiment, and in doing so have every confidence " that wherever it may be called upon to maintain " the honour of England they will be borne with " that gallantry which is at all times displayed by " the British army."

Chapter XII.

1862. West Indies Raising the 4th W.I. Regt.

In November, 1862, orders were received at Nassau that a 4th West India Regiment was to be raised, and that each of the three West India Regiments were to contribute two companies to the new regiment, thereby reducing the number of companies from 10 to 8, but with an establishment of officers for 10 companies; also that in future one entire regiment would be stationed on the West Coast of Africa where the period of service was to be limited to three, instead of four years, and further, that the six companies of the 2nd West India Regiment would be at once relieved by the 3rd West India Regiment from Jamaica on which the 2nd West India would be distributed as follows :—

1862. 4 companies (head-quarters) at Barbados.

1 company	....	....	,, Trinidad.
2 companies	....	....	,, Demerara.
1 company	....	....	,, Berbice.

—

Total, 8 companies

Vide Horse Guards' Letter, 10/10/62.

Disbandment of Gold Coast Artillery and raising 5th W.I. Regt.

In consequence of a serious mutiny in the Gold Coast Artillery it was decided by Horse-Guards' letter, dated 17th February, 1863, to disband that corps and to raise a fifth West India Regiment for service on the west coast of Africa, by which means there would be two regiments stationed on the west coast of Africa.

West Indies, 1863.

On the 7th April, 1863, Nos. 4 and 8 companies 2nd West India Regiment embarked on board H.M.S. "*Adventure*" with the following officers, viz., Captains Willcocks and Knapp, Lieuts. Eyre and Cooper, arriving at Barbados on the 30th.

On the 20th September, 1863, Nos. 5 and 6 companies embarked at Sierra Leone on board H.M.S. "*Megœra*" with the following officers, viz., Lieuts. Walsh and Brett, and Ensign Herbert. No. 5 company was landed at Demerara, and No. 6 company at Trinidad. On the 17th November, the head-quarters, with Nos. 1 and 2 companies, embarked at Nassau on board H.M.S. "*Megœra*" with the following officers for Barbados:—Colonel Whitfeild, Major Mends, Captain Reece, Lieuts. Williams, Matthews, Hall, Turton (Adjutant),

1863. From Nassau to Barbados. Head-quarters with Nos. 1, 2, 4, 8 Cos. December, 1863

Rogers, Ross; Ensign Hopkins; Staff.-Asst.-Surgeons Greig and Boulton.

On passing Jamaica, 22nd November, the volunteers from the regiment for the 4th West India Regiment were landed. On the 8th December, the troops put into the island of St. Vincent, this being the first time the regiment visited that island since its departure in 1797, two years after being raised there.

Distribution.

On the 10th December they arrived at Barbados. The regiment was now distributed as follows:—

Head-quarters and Nos. 2, 4 and 8 Barbados, Nos. 3 and 7 on the Gold Coast, No. 5 at Demerara, No. 6 at Trinidad.

Gold Coast. Nos. 3 and 7 Companies retained for service.

In consequence of the threatening attitude of the Ashantis, Nos. 3 and 7 companies, stationed at Anamaboe, were retained when the 4th West India Regiment arrived to relieve the 2nd in August, 1863.

Second Ashanti War.

This detachment was under command of Captain Knox, until he was invalided in March, 1863: Captain Williams succeeding—he in turn was invalided in August, 1863. By the 29th of that month, all the officers serving with the detachment had either died or were invalided, and two officers of the 4th West India (Captain Edwards and Lieut. Barry) were detailed for duty with the detachment.

The duties were most arduous, the detachment during that unhealthy season being constantly on outpost duty, on the borders of the protectorate; their soldier-like good conduct called forth, unsolicited, the following, which is an extract of a

1863. **Gold Coast. Second Ashanti War.** letter from Governor Pine to Lieut.-Colonel Conran, commanding troops, Gold Coast :—

" Government House, Cape Coast,

" 30th October, 1863.

" I take this opportunity of recording the " esteem in which I hold the services performed by " companies of the 2nd West India Regiment " (whose good deeds are already known to me) " while attached to this Government, under " circumstances of peculiar difficulty, privations, " and hardships which I witnessed with sorrowful " admiration: deeply regretting that I am power- " less to do ought but express my gratitude: and " request that you, Sir, will do me the favour to " forward a copy of this letter with those you " propose transmitting to His Royal Highness on " same subject."

Reinforcements 1864. **West Indies. Nos. 4, 6 and 8 Companies to Jamaica.** In consequence of a strong detachment of the 1st West India being ordered from Jamaica as reinforcement for the Gold Coast, the 2nd West India was ordered to furnish three companies to take their place at Jamaica; accordingly, on the 8th February, 1864, H.M.S. "*Tamar*" took on board Nos. 4 and 8 companies and proceeding to Trinidad, embarked No. 6 and proceeded to Jamaica: the following officers accompanying the detachment—Major Mends, Captain Fanning, Lieuts. Lowry, Ness, and Rogers, Ensigns MacGregor and Phelps.

1864. **Officers for Gold Coast.** The following officers proceeded to Africa with the 1st West India to join Nos. 3 and 7 companies on the Gold Coast:—

Captain Reece, Lieuts. Williams and Hall, Ensign Tongue, arriving at Cape Coast on the 9th

1864. Officers for Gold Coast.

April, Lieut. Doithie having previously arrived there.

The expeditionary force was now composed of the following troops :—

	Officers.	Men.
1st West India - -	11 - - - -	300
2nd ,, ,, - -	5 - - - -	170
3rd ,, ,, - -	6 - - - -	170
4th ,, ,, - -	30 - - - -	850
5th ,, ,, - -	4 - - - -	10
Total - - - -	56	1,500

The troops were kept for the most part on outpost duty, the intention being to remain on the defensive until about July, when the rains would be less severe, and then to make an advance on Coomassie.

The season being an unusually unhealthy one, the troops suffered most severely, especially from want of proper shelter from the heavy rains.

The losses from climate were so disastrous, that early in June, orders from home were sent out to the Colonial Government that all operations against the Ashantis were to cease, and notifying that the extra troops (1st and 2nd W.I.) would be withdrawn. It took some time bringing in the different outposts. The transport "*Wambojeez*" arrived at Cape Coast on the 27th July, the troops embarked on the 30th and sailed next day for Barbados.

1864. Ashanti War. Nos. 3 and 7 Companies.

The following officers embarked with Nos. 3 and 7 companies, Captain Reece, Lieuts. Williams and Doithie, and Ensign Tongue; Lieut. Hall having been invalided.

The following letter was published in General Orders, Cape Coast Castle, 28th July, 1864:

" Government House, 27th July, 1864.

" Sir,

" On the eve of the departure of the detach- " ments 1st and 2nd West India Regiments, which " have been annexed to your command on my " requisition since April last, I request that you " will be pleased to permit me, through you, to " record my thanks, as governor of these Settle- " ments, for the services they have performed " conjointly with yourself and regiment.

Nos. 3 & 7 Companies

" I feel I have been the means of imposing " upon her Majesty's troops, laborious, ungracious " and apparently thankless duty; but my inten- " tions and motives have been so fully, and I trust " satisfactorily discussed throughout Great Britain " that I dare hope that the officers and men will " believe that I invited them to participate in a " constitutional measure, which I am convinced " would add to their military reputation and " honour.

" To the decision of her Majesty's Govern- " ment as to its altered policy, we are all compelled " to bow, and it only remains for me to express my " regret to every officer and man of the 1st and " 2nd West India Regiments for the natural and " laudable disappointment which they have " experienced in not being engaged in more active " military operations, and to tender my heartfelt " thanks for the prompt and ready obedience with

1864. Ashanti War. "which they responded to my call on behalf of our "Royal Mistress, and for their patient endurance "under extraordinary trial. . . . .

" (Signed) RICHARD PINE,

"To Hon. Col. Conran, Governor & C.-in-Chief.
" Commanding Troops."

The "*Wambojeez*" arrived at Barbados on the 3rd December, 1864. Nos. 3 and 7 companies disembarked and joined head-quarters.

West Indies. Cos. called by letters instead of numbers. Distribution of Regiment 1864.

The method of naming the companies was changed at the end of 1864 from "numbers" to "letters," and at Christmas, 1864, the regiment was distributed as follows:—

Barbados -	Head-quarters and A, B, C, G Co's.
Honduras - - - -	D and H Co's.
Demerara - - - -	E and F Co's.

1865. Jamaica Rebellion.

In consequence of an excessive drought throughout Jamaica, which caused a scarcity of food almost amounting to a famine, an opportunity was afforded to political agitators to excite the peasantry.

A native named Gordon presided over a public meeting held in Kingston, at which a resolution was passed, "calling upon all the "descendants of Africa in every parish throughout "the island to form themselves into societies and "hold public meetings and to co-operate, for the "purpose of setting forth their grievances." Shortly after this, on the 11th October, 1865, the vestry of St. Thomas-in-the-East met for usual business. At about 3 o'clock, some hundreds of people armed with cutlasses, sticks, muskets and bayonets, entered the square in front of the Court

1865. Jamaica Rebellion. House at Morant Bay, and "declared for war." They were all blacks, and their cry was "colour "for colour, blood for blood."

They began by stoning a guard of volunteers which was drawn up. The Riot Act was read and the volunteers fired, but were soon overpowered.

A hand-to-hand struggle ensued, during which the commander of the volunteers, Captain Hitchens, was hacked to death. All the officers and many of the members of the volunteer corps nobly died at their posts, doing their duty.

The custos of the parish, the Curate of Bath, the inspector of police, and a number of magistrates and other persons were also murdered.

Martial law was at once proclaimed, and all available troops called out. H.M.S. "*Urgent*" was sent to Barbados to request assistance.

The ship arrived at 5 p.m. on the 23rd October, and at 7 p.m. orders were received for the head-quarters and four companies (A, B, C and G) 2nd West India Regiment to embark at 6 a.m. next day, as well as two companies the Buffs, and half (½) battery R.A. to embark at the same time.

This was done, and the "*Urgent*" was under weigh with 600 troops on board at 9 a.m. 24th and arrived at Port Royal, Jamaica, on the evening of the 28th October.

The Buffs were landed at once, and the "*Urgent*" proceeded on the morning of the 30th to the following ports in the western district, landing detachments of the regiment and R.A., viz., Port Maria, Dry Harbour, Falmouth (where head-

1865. Jamaica Rebellion.

quarters were disembarked), Montego Bay, and Lucea. This district was designated the "western district," and was placed under command of Col. Whitfeild.

The measures taken by the Government had the desired result, and the rebellion did not spread into the western district as was feared.

The rebellion had been practically crushed before the arrival of the regiment, as Boyle, the ringleader, was captured on the 23rd October, and tried and hanged on the 24th : while Gordon, who was the principal agitator, was tried by court-martial on the 21st, and was also hanged on the 24th ; but there was an uneasy feeling for some time, as although crushed it was still smouldering, and would have come to life again, except for the presence of troops moving about the country.

The troops suffered considerable hardships, owing to the absence of all proper accommodation, being supplied with one blanket only, having to put up in sheds, barns, &c., exposed to the heavy rains usual at that time of the year.

The following officers were employed in this work :—

Colonel Whitfeild, Bt.-Major Reece, Capts. Drouet, Wise and Knapp, Lieuts. Brett, Turton (Adjt.), Rogers, Cooper, Last, Dolan, Ensigns Stainforth, Mitchell, Grant, Pay-Master Ternau, Staff-Surgeon Crisp, Staff-Asst.-Surgeon Byrne.

By the end of the year all trace of rebellion was stamped out.

1866. **Change of distribution of Regiment: Left Wing to Gold Coast, Head-quarters to Nassau.**

Early in 1866, orders were received for a general change of stations in the West Indies and West Africa.

On the 30th March, H.M.S. "*Urgent*" arrived at Falmouth, embarked B and C companies, proceeded to Honduras, where D and H companies were embarked, and from there to Cape Coast Castle, arriving on the 31st May, relieving the 4th West India Regiment.

The following officers moved over with the left wing—Lieut.-Colonel Dunlop, Captains Drouet, Wise, Hall; Lieuts. Brett, Lowry, Phelps, Sayce, Last, Dolan; Ensigns Hartford, Hamilton and Warner.

West Africa Garrison. 1½ Battalions.

Detachments were stationed at Accra and Lagos. Later in the year, the 1st West India arrived from the West Indies, and was divided as follows, head-quarters and four companies at Sierra Leone, and four companies at Gambia.

West Indies Jamaica. 1866.

On the 24th August, the head-quarters and four companies moved from Falmouth to Up Park Camp.

Inspection.

On the 28th August, the regiment was inspected by M.-General O'Connor.

Head-quarters to Nassau.

The head-quarters and four companies—A, E, F, G—moved to Nassau, embarking in H.M.S. "*Urgent*," on the 27th November, arriving at Nassau on the 4th December, 1866.

They remained there without alteration till June, 1869.

1867. **Pram-Pram Expedition.**

In August, 1867, a serious disturbance occurred at Mumford, a town between Cape Coast and Accra, and a party of the 2nd West India Regiment was despatched under Lieut. Ness to establish order.

In October, 1867, the Egbas threatened to invade Lagos, and the detachment, under command of Bt.-Major Molesworth, was moved to the frontier.

In the same month (October) a detachment under command of Lieut. Ness was employed in arresting some chiefs at Pram-Pram; it was so satisfactorily managed that the thanks of the Colonial Office was conveyed through the Horse Guards in the following letter from the Military Secretary to the officer commanding troops.

"The attention of the Field Marshal "Commanding-in-Chief having been drawn to a "despatch received at the Colonial Office from the "Administrator-in-Chief of the West African "Settlements, containing very favourable accounts "of the conduct of Lieut. Bolton, 1st West India "Regiment (acting district commissioner) and "Lieut. (now Captain) Ness (then 2nd W.I. Regt.) "and the troops under his command, on a recent "expedition to some chiefs at Pram-Pram and "Mango, on the Gold Coast: I am directed to "acquaint you that his Royal Highness considers "the report to be highly satisfactory, and I have "to request that you will express to the officers "and troops employed on the service in question, "His Royal Highness's approval of the manner in "which they carried out the very difficult duties "they had to perform."

1868. West Indies. Col. Whitfeild leaves the Regt. after over 40 years' service. Col. W. Hill to command.

On the 14th February, 1868, Col. Whitfeild completed forty years' service in the regiment, and was entertained at dinner by the officers of the regiment in commemoration.

He retired from the regiment on promotion to Major-General, on the 28th October, 1868, and Colonel William Hill succeeded to the command, Major Mends, who was serving in command of Wing, on Gold Coast, obtaining promotion to junior Lieut.-Colonel.

189. Disbandment of 4th W.I. Regt.

In February, 1869, it was decided to disband the 4th West India, and orders were issued for the Wing, 2nd West India, serving on the Gold Coast, to be held in readiness to proceed to Barbados, and all arrangements for an immediate move were made, but the order as far as related to the Wing was cancelled on the 12th November, 1869.

In the meantime, the 4th West India was disbanded on the 1st April, 1869, one company letter "I" being added to each of the three remaining West India Regiments.

Head-quarters move from Nassau to Barbados, June

In pursuance of the original order for the move, head-quarters and one company moved in H.M.S. "*Barracouta*" on the 2nd June, *via* Jamaica to Barbados, leaving three companies at Nassau, arriving at Barbados on the 6th August, 1869.

Distribution of Regiment, August.

The regiment was now distributed as follows:—

Head-quarters and one company at Barbados (F).

Three companies at Nassau (A.E.G.)

One company (the new "I" Co.) at Demerara; and the Left Wing on the Gold Coast.

1870.
Disbandment of 3rd W.I. Regt.

On the 2nd March, 1870, further alterations were ordered as regards the garrison of the West Coast, by the reduction of the 3rd West India, with orders that the 1st West India was to move to West Indies, and that the companies of the 2nd West India on the Gold Coast were to be relieved by two companies of the corps from the West Indies, and that two other companies were to be stationed at Sierra Leone. Troops being withdrawn from all stations except Cape Coast Castle and Sierra Leone. Head-quarters of both regiments to be stationed in the West Indies.

In consequence of the fresh order, head-quarters and one company moved from Barbados to Demerara on the 11th April, 1870, in H.M.S. "*Danae*."

1870.
West Indies and West Africa.

Two companies, "D" and "H," arrived at Demerara from the Gold Coast on the 18th of June, in H.M.S. "*Orontes*" *via* Nassau, having three companies from that station on board. Embarked "I" company and proceeded to Sierra Leone, disembarked two companies at Sierra Leone early in August, proceeded to Cape Coast Castle, relieved the two companies stationed there on the 24th August, and proceeded with them to Barbados, arriving there in September, 1870.

Distribution.

The regiment was now distributed as follows:—

Demerara head-quarters and three companies D, F, and H.

Barbados, two companies, B and C.

Sierra Leone, two companies, A and E.

Cape Coast, two companies, G and I.

1870. Lt.-Col. Harley retires. Lt.-Col. Wise to command.

Lieut.-Colonel Harley was appointed to the command of the regiment on the 7th May, 1870; he retired on 19th October, 1872, and Lieut.-Colonel Wise assumed the command from that date.

No change took place in the West Indies until June, 1873.

Nothing of special interest occurred on the Gold Coast until 1873.

Gold Coast. Ashanti War.

In 1870 the King of Ashanti claimed Elmina, and protested against its being handed over to the English by the Dutch.

After considerable correspondence the transfer was at length completed on the 6th April, 1872, notwithstanding the angry protest of the Ashantis. For some months negotiations went on with respect to rent and ransom for European prisoners, held by the Ashantis, but without any satisfactory result.

On the 4th February, 1873, information was received at Cape Coast Castle that the Ashantis had crossed the Prah 12,000 strong, and were advancing on the Coast in three divisions.

The garrison of the Gold Coast consisted of two (2) companies, 2nd West India, under command of Captain Turton, with a total strength of 167: these were considered not more than sufficient to guard the different Castles on the Coast, and consequently arms and ammunition were issued to the Fanti Army, and they went out towards the frontier to meet the Ashantis, which they did on the 8th April, resulting in the Fantees holding their ground, and the Ashanti advance being checked; however, on the 14th, the Ashantis

1873. Ashanti War.

attacked and drove the Fantees back, the fight lasting from 10 a.m. till 7 p.m.

The Fantees continued to retire before the Ashanti advance, until on the 5th June, 1873, when they were attacked at Jonquah and entirely routed. The Ashantis occupying the village of Effootoo, about 12 miles distant from Cape Coast, and 15 miles from Elmina.

On the 7th June, Lieut.-Colonel Festing landed with 110 marines and assumed command of the troops.

A company in the meantime had reinforced the regiment from Sierra Leone, and brought up the strength of the detachment, 2nd West India to 9 officers, and 262 n.c.o.'s and men. The officers then present were Captains Forbes, Brett, Turton, Matthews, Haynes, Grant; Lieuts. Des Barres, Hopkins and Pollard.

Engagement at Elmina 13th June

Immediate steps were now taken to put Cape Coast Castle and Elmina into a state of defence. This had to be commenced by destroying a large part of Elmina, which was occupied by people friendly to the Ashantis. While this was going on a force of Ashantis, estimated at 2,000 advanced to attack the British. Colonel Festing, who was present, directed that the troops were to remain on the defensive, considering they were not strong enough to go out and attack the Ashantis; however, "E" company, 2nd West India, seeing the enemy a couple of hundred yards in front of them, and at the moment no officer being present with them, they determined to disregard the order, and charged the enemy with such spirit that they drove them back, killing a large number.

Sergeant and Bugler.

1873. Ashanti War. Engagement at Elmina, 13th June.

Seeing this, Lieut. Wells, R.N., came up with the Barracouta men, attacked the enemy in flank, and completed the rout; in this engagement one man, 2nd West India, was wounded, and 250 Ashantis were killed.

This action resulted in making the Ashantis keep their distance.

By the 18th of June the main body of the Ashanti army had established itself at Beulah, about 7 miles from Cape Coast Castle. Estimated strength, 20,000 men.

The whole of the marines were invalided home during the first week in August.

1873. Ashanti War Head-quarters proceed to Africa. Arrived 6th July.

The head-quarters and B, C, D and H companies embarked at Demerara and Barbados on the 16th June, and arrived at Cape Coast Castle on the 6th July, with the following officers:—

Lieut.-Colonel Wise, Major Russell, Captain Lowry; Lieuts. Warner, Jones, Devereux, Dalgleish (Adjutant), Brooks; Sub.-Lieuts. Filliter, Patchett, Keighley; Pay-master Moore; Qr.-Master Harper; and 360 non-commissioned officers and men.

On the 29th July the Ashantis made a raid against the Aguafoos, and came within 2½ miles of Elmina.

At the same time a large Ashanti army, estimated at 12,000, occupied the country round Axim, threatening the Fort.

During August that detachment of 2nd West India was constantly employed in small skirmishes, and by the middle of August the Ashantis had invested Dixcove and Secondee as well.

1873.
Ashanti War.

In the early part of September information was received that a strong expeditionary force was to be raised locally, and that Sir G. Wolseley and a large number of special service officers were coming out to superintend it. In consequence of this the Governor, Colonel Harley, after conferring with the naval and military heads at Cape Coast Castle, decided not to make any offensive movement, which might not coincide with the arrangements of the new commander of the expeditionary force.

On the 2nd October Sir G. Wolseley and Staff arrived and at once commenced their attempt to raise native levies, and to make a road to the Prah.

Chapter XIII.

1873.
Ashanti War,
Engagement at
Essarman,
14th October.

On the 14th October the first offensive movement was made by an attack on the enemy's camp at Essarman, in which 200 2nd West India were engaged. This expedition was under the command of Lieut.-Col. Wood, V.C., Sir G. Wolseley and Staff accompanying the expedition. The village was captured and destroyed, the British loss being 32 wounded. The force then returned to Elmina, *via* Anquama, Akimfoo and Ampene; all of these places were destroyed, the ground covered being 22 miles. Captain Forbes was wounded.

Napoleon, Accroful, Abra Crampa and Dunquah were now occupied by small detachments of the regiment; Captain Brett and 40 men at Accroful, and Captain Haynes and 100 men at Dunquah.

On the 27th October the Ashantis broke up their camp at Mampon.

1873. **Action of Asianchi 27th October.**

On the same day Colonel Festing made a reconnaissance in force towards the Ashanti camp of Asianchi, taking besides irregulars, 100 2nd West India, with the following officers: Captain Haynes, Lieuts. Jones, Filliter, and Sub.-Lieut. Patchett.

They surprised the advanced camp, and the Ashantis bolted, but, soon recovering their panic, returned, and attacked the British.

" The war drums began to beat almost " instantly, and in five minutes a heavy fire was " opened upon us from the bush which surrounded " the camp. This, fortunately, stood on high " ground, affording a good position for defence; " and a heavy fire was opened in return upon the " bush, from which a perfect rain of slugs proceeded " from an invisible foe. The Annamaboo men " stood their ground gallantly, and the West " Indians behaved with great coolness; but the " majority of our native allies were by no means " conspicuous for their pluck. . . . The fight " lasted for an hour and a half, and as it was then " getting late in the afternoon, and there was no " possibility of attacking the enemy in their strong- " hold, the bush, Colonel Festing determined to fall " back on Dunquah, which he did unmolested." (*Henty*). In this engagement five officers were wounded, including Capt. Haynes and Lieut. Filliter.

It was now quite evident that the Ashanti Army was preparing to retire from Elmina to the Prah.

Reconnaissance from Dunquah.

On the 3rd November Colonel Festing again made a reconnaissance towards the Ashanti camp, and started with 83 2nd West India, about 900 native allies, and some Houssas with rockets, under Lieut. Eardley Wilmot, R.A.

1873. Reconnaissance from Dunquah.

" When we approached the Ashanti camp the " alarm was given and the fight began almost at " once. The bush was extremely dense, and from " it the enemy poured a terrible fire.

" Only about 100 of the native allies stood " firm, and even these fired in the wildest and most " useless manner ; the rest, headed by the King of " Dunquah, took flight and did not stop until they " reached the camp at Dunquah. The West Indians " behaved with great steadiness and gallantry, and " kept up for two hours a heavy snider fire at their " invisible foe." (*Henty*).

Lieut. Wilmot, R.A., advanced beyond the line of fire, and was working his rocket tube with great success when he was seen to fall, on which Lieut. Jones ran out and carried him in on his back, but as he reached the firing line he was struck in the hip by a bullet and knocked over ; on this Lieut.-Colonel Festing pulled Lieut. Wilmot in behind the line, but too late to save his life.

Colonel Festing, finding that the enemy were endeavouring to cut off his retreat, now fell back upon Dunquah. In this engagement one officer was killed (Lieut. Wilmot) and four wounded, including Lieut. Jones severely, and Lieut. Patchett slightly.

Lt.-Col. Webber takes over command.

Lieut.-Colonel Webber having arrived from England on the 2nd November, assumed command of the regiment, and marched with the Headquarters for Mansu on the 3rd.

Action of Abra Crampa 5th and 6th November.

On the 5th of November 93 men, under command of Captain Grant, formed the principal portion of the garrison of Abra Crampa when it was attacked in force by the enemy ; the attack was almost a surprise. " A heavy fire broke out

1873. Action of Abra Crampa. 5th and 6th November.

"suddenly upon the left flank of the position, and "the picquets came running in saying that the "whole Ashanti army was upon them; there was a "moment of haste, but none of confusion. Every "officer had his allotted place, and even the natives, "encouraged by the calmness of the officers, by the "presence of white troops (marines), and of the men "of the 2nd West India Regiment, took up their "posts with steadiness and alacrity. Everything "was in readiness for the defence; the ground for "100 yards had been cleared of trees and under-"growth, and, indeed, at most points, the band of "open ground was considerably wider than this. "The church at the top of the village was loop-"holed and held by sailors and marines; the men "could fire from the body, from the gallery, and "from the roof. From this point they could not "only repel any direct attack upon the church, but "sweep the approaches on two sides of the village. "Shelter trenches had been run along outside the "lines of the village; the huts were all loop-holed, "and connected by bamboo fences." . . .

(*Henty*).

The enemy kept up a heavy fire from the bush, doing little damage, but would not advance across the open. The attack commenced at half-past three in the afternoon, but the fire slackened for a short time at about five o'clock. Shortly before dark a furious fire was again opened, and the vigilance of the besieged was redoubled. From 6 o'clock till midnight the fire was kept up without intermission on either side, after which a dropping fire was maintained by both sides till 4 a.m. About an hour later Captain Brett came in from Accroful with a reinforcement of 50 2nd West India. Scouts were sent out, and it was found that the enemy had retired to their camp; at 9 o'clock they again pressed on to the attack, which was carried on in the same manner as the previous day.

1873. Action of Abra Crampa, 5th and 6th November.

"The 2nd West India made several very plucky "charges, drove the enemy out of a clump of "bushes in advance of the wood, and shot many of "them down." (*Henty*).

During one of these sorties they were cheered by the sailors and marines, who held the church.

After this engagement the enemy retreated to the Prah, and for two days they were, unfortunately, allowed to do so unmolested. On the 8th Captain Bromhead with some Houssas, Kossos, and Abra men, followed up the enemy, harassing their rear. At last this force came up with the main body of the Ashantis' rear guard, which turned and opened fire upon the pursuers, who, after a short time, became utterly disorganised, and fled in the wildest confusion, numbers being shot and hacked down. Forty-five headless bodies were found on the road a few days after.

After this experience of native allies, they were disbanded and their arms taken from them, and they were pressed into service as carriers and labourers.

Fazoo Rear Guard. Action 27th Nov.

Colonel Wood, with his native regiment and 50 2nd West India, under command of Sub.-Lieut. Patchett, now took up the pursuit and came up with the enemy's rear guard on the 27th November; the enemy opened a tremendous fire on them. For some little time the British held their own, until it became evident that the Ashantis were trying to out-flank them and cut off their retreat, upon which it was determined to retire, the 2nd West India covering the retreat. This was carried out steadily, until, meeting a body of carriers bringing up stores, &c., they, seeing the troops retreating, were panic-struck, and fled, throwing down their loads; the panic communicated

1873. Fazoo Rear Guard, Action, 27th Nov.

itself to Wood's regiment, who joined in the stampede; the 2nd West India, however, were quite steady, and keeping up a heavy musketry fire on the enemy, effected their retreat in good order, none being killed, and only a few wounded.

The Ashantis did not pursue their advantage, but carried out their retreat across the Prah.

On the 29th November, Lieut. Bell, Sub-Lieuts. Trist and Caulfeild arrived from England and reached head-quarters at Mansu on the 4th December.

Privates Fagan & Lewis plucky reconnaissance

About this time news came that the Ashantis were thoroughly disheartened, and were crossing the Prah as quickly as they could. On the 9th, Sir G. Wolseley wishing to ascertain the truth of this, "called for a volunteer to go and "discover whether the Ashantis were all across. "Two men, 2nd West India, Privates Fagan and "Lewis, at once volunteered, and went on alone, "25 miles to the Prah. They found that large "numbers of dead lay by the path along its whole "distance, and that at Prahsu there were very "many dead. The survivors had all crossed. The "soldiers wrote their names on a piece of paper "and fastened it to a tree to prove that they had "been there; fired their rifles in derision across the "stream, and returned to Akrofoum with the news. "This feat appears to me one of the most "courageous, if not the most courageous, which "was performed during the whole campaign. "Nothing can be imagined more trying to the "nerves than that long march through the lonely "and irksome forests, with the knowledge that at "any moment some body of Ashantis who had "lingered behind the rest might spring out upon "them, and that if not killed at once they were

Privates Fagan & Lewis plucky reconnaisance.

"doomed to a lingering death by torture at "Coomassie." (*Henty*).

For the above services the General Officer commanding, rewarded each of them with a gratuity of five pounds, and at the conclusion of the campaign they each received a medal for distinguished conduct in the field.

1874. Prah.

On the 1st January the regiment marched out of Mansu and reached the Prah on the 3rd January. On the same day some Ambassadors came in from Ashanti to treat; and one of them, on seeing the preparation made for attacking his country, committed suicide, preferring that, to being the bearer of bad tidings back to his King.

On the 5th Lord Gifford, in command of the scouts, partly composed of men of the 2nd West India, crossed the Prah, and advanced as far as Essiaman, 13 miles, where he came in touch with the enemy. At this time the transport entirely broke down, and the men were placed on half rations, and were employed for a week in carrying provisions and ammunition from Yan Coomassie to the Prah, a distance of 10 miles. This duty the men volunteered for, and did it cheerfully and well.

The breakdown was of a most serious nature, and this action on their part had a most important influence on the future of the campaign.

On the 12th January an advanced party of 28 non-commissioned officers and men, under command of Lieutenant Jones, who was hardly fit for work after his recent wound, crossed the Prah with "Russell's" regiment, and moved with them to Adansi.

1874. Cross the Prah.

On the following day, 13th, two hundred and nine men, under command of Lieut.-Colonel Webber, with Captains Haynes, Paterson, and Grant; Lieuts. Des Barres, Filliter, and Sub-Lieutenant Caulfeild, marched towards Pericomie, arriving there on the 20th. This was a most trying march, as in addition to their kits, 3 days' rations, 70 rounds of ammunition, and blankets, each section of five men had to carry one box of ammunition and one *tente d'abri*. Only two stretchers were allowed for the whole party. After a halt of seven days there, an advance was made over the Adansi hills into Ashanti proper, and Foomanah was reached on the 27th.

Cross the Adansi.

By this time most of the force was concentrated at Queesa and Foomanah, the latter being about half-a-mile to the front.

On the 29th January, all the troops were ordered to be ready at 5 a.m. to march off on getting the word; the 2nd West India marched off at about 8 a.m. as the rear battalion of the column.

Insarfu.

Insarfu was reached on the 30th. The European troops at once pushed on through Quarman to Amoaful, fighting their way.

Insarfu was now made the base, and it became the duty of the 2nd West India to escort ammunition and provisions to the front. On the 31st a party of 60 men, under command of Captain Grant and Sub.-Lieut. Caulfeild, occupied Quarman, the Head-quarters of the regiment moving on to Amoaful on the 1st February.

Quarman. Amoaful.

The ration of rum, the issue of which had been stopped on the 8th January, was now resumed.

1874. Fall of Coomassie.

The army reached and took possession of Coomassie on the 4th February; the only men of the 2nd West India who actually entered were those under command of Lieut. Jones, and the scouts under Lord Gifford.

Great was the disappointment felt at Amoaful and Quarman when the news arrived that Coomassie had fallen, and that the regiment which had borne the brunt of the campaign for over eight months, were not allowed to participate in the honour of entering it; the regiment deserved better treatment than it got on this occasion.

Between the 30th January and the 4th February the regiment was constantly employed as above stated on convoy duty and patrolling. There were few casualties, but many narrow escapes. One man, Private Morrison, was wounded, and afterwards had his head cut off while on reconnoitring duty. Captain Paterson and Sub.-Lieut. Caulfeild, with about 50 men, were fired into on the night of the 31st January while escorting one thousand carriers from Insarfu to Quarman; the carriers at once dropped their loads and bolted; the 2nd West India returned the fire by a few steady volleys, aiming at the flash caused by the enemy's rifles, and after the enemy had been dispersed took up as many of the loads as they could carry, and brought them into Quarman, making several trips. A few men were slightly wounded, but several had narrow escapes; two men had their rifle barrels damaged by enemy's bullets striking them, and Captain Paterson got a bullet through his helmet.

Return March to the Coast.

The regiment remained at Amoaful until the 8th February, when the return march to the coast was commenced.

1874. **Return March to the Coast.**

Fifty men, under command of Sub.-Lieut. Caulfeild, formed an escort for the General Officer commanding, moving with the Head-quarters of the Army until it reached Mansu, when their services were dispensed with.

The regiment reached Inquabim, 12 miles from Cape Coast, on the 25th February, and on account of the crowded state of Cape Coast remained there until the 6th March, when they marched into Cape Coast and encamped at Connors' and Prospect Hills.

Farewell. General Orders

On the 3rd March, 1874, the following General Order (No. 43) was published :

" Before leaving for England the Major-" General commanding wishes to convey to the " soldiers of the 1st and 2nd West India regiments " his appreciation of their soldier-like qualities, " and of the manner in which they have performed " their duty during the recent campaign.

" Portions of the 2nd West India have been " in every affair of the war and the regiment " generally has undergone fatigues and exposure " in a most creditable manner.

" When owing to desertion of the carriers the " transport difficulties became serious, the men of " both these regiments responded most cheerfully " to the call made upon them, and by daily carry-" ing loads helped to relieve the force from its then " most pressing difficulty.

" In saying good-bye, the Major-General " assures them he will always remember with pride " and pleasure that he had the honour of com-" manding men whose loyalty to their Queen, and " whose soldier-like qualities have been so well

1874. Farewell General Orders.

"proved in the war now so happily at an end."

By command,

(Signed) J. W. BAKER, Major A.A.G.

Regiments embarked for Sierra Leone.

On the 19th March the regiment embarked on board the transport "*Nebraska*," and remained off Cape Coast waiting for orders to proceed to the West Indies, which, not arriving by the mail, the ship was ordered to proceed to Sierra Leone on the 24th, arriving there on the 31st, and two companies were landed to relieve the over-crowded ship, where they remained until orders from England arrived on the 17th April, and the transport sailed for the West Indies on the 19th.

During the wait at Sierra Leone, two officers, Lt.-Col. Webber and Sub.-Lieut. Caulfeild were invalided to England on the 18th April. Twenty-three men, two women, and two children died of pneumonia during the fortnight they lay off Sierra Leone, the ship was over-crowded and badly fitted for the tropics.

Officers who served in the Campaign.

The following officers served in the campaign :—

Lt.-Col.	WISE	....	Invalided
,,	WEBBER	....	Invalided from Sierra Leone
Major	BRAVO	....	Invalided
,,	RUSSELL	....	Invalided
Captain	FORBES	....	Invalided
,,	BRETT	....	Invalided
,,	LANYON	....	Invalided

1874.
Officers who served in the campaign.

Captain	TURTON	....	Invalided
,,	MATHEWS	....	Invalided
,,	HAYNES	....	To West Indies
,,	LOWRY	....	Invalided
,,	PATERSON	....	To West Indies
,,	GRANT	...	Remained at Sierra Leone as A. D. C. to Gov.
,,	FOWLER	....	Invalided
Lieut.	DESBARRES	....	To West Indies
,,	WARNER	....	Died
,,	JONES	....	To West Indies
,,	STOKER	....	Invalided
,,	HOPKINS	....	Died
,,	POLLARD	....	Invalided
,,	BROOKS	....	Invalided
,,	DALGLEISH (Adjt.)		Died
,,	BELL	....	Invalided
,,	DEVEREUX	....	Invalided
,,	WILKIN	....	To West Indies
Sub.-Lt.	FILLITER	....	To West Indies
,,	PATCHETT	....	Invalided
,,	KEIGHLEY	....	To West Indies
,,	TRIST	....	Invalided
,,	CAULFEILD	.. .	Invalided from Sierra Leone
Pay.-Mr.	MOORE	....	To West Indies
Qr.-Mr.	HARPER	....	Invalided

1874. Ashanti War.

The under-mentioned officers arrived at Cape Coast in February, but did not get the medal, having arrived after hostilities were ended: —Sub.-Lieuts. Cox, Masters, Foster, Grant, Stanley, Doyle, Lyster, Tyndale, Kerans, of whom Sub.-Lieut. Stanley was invalided, and Sub.-Lieut. Cox died a few weeks after leaving the Coast.

Chapter XIV.

1874.
Sails for West Indies.

On the 19th April, 1874, the regiment sailed for the West Indies, arriving at Barbados on the 8th May, disembarking on the 9th. On landing the regiment was presented with a congratulatory address from the people of Barbados, after which they marched to Queen's House, where they were addressed by the Governor and the General Officer commanding, and then to St. Ann's Barracks, where the men were entertained at a dinner, provided by the Legislative Council.

A Ball was given in honour of the officers on the 11th May, and on the 12th the Head-quarters and six companies embarked on s.s. "*Nebraska*," and sailed for Jamaica, leaving "H" and "I" companies at Barbados.

Head-quarters arrived at Jamaica 19th May. Address of Welcome.

They arrived and disembarked at Kingston on the 19th, when the following address was presented by the Custos of the Parish.

"To Lieut.-Colonel Webber or other officer "commanding, and to the officers, non-commis- "sioned officers and men of H.M.'s 2nd West India "Regiment."

1874. Head-quarters arrived at Jamaica, 19th May. Address of welcome.

" We, the Custos, Magistrates and Citizens " of Kingston, unite in welcoming you on your " return from the arduous and dangerous campaign " in which you have been engaged in Ashanti.

" To the patient endurance and daring " courage of Her Majesty's forces in this expedition " do we owe the fresh victories achieved, and " further prestige added to the British arms " engaged in the war from beginning to end, des- " pising all danger and fatigue, under almost insur- " mountable difficulties; and with an energy and " courage not to be surpassed you nobly performed " your duty as soldiers.

" With delight and pride we heard that at a " critical period of the campaign, when, through " desertion of the native allies, the transport broke " down, and the briefest period of inaction would " have jeopardized the success of the entire " expedition, the men of the West India regiments " nobly volunteered to take this work upon their " shoulders, and with patience and endurance per- " formed the toilsome task.

" But for the ready performance of this im- " portant service, most disastrous results might " have ensued, and the enterprize at this stage " must have been abandoned.

" Your gallant comrades in arms have returned " to England, been received with loud plaudits " of the nation, and honoured by acknowledg- " ments of gratitude from our gracious Sovereign " in person. Duty requires your return to this " part of Her Majesty's dominions, and we, as " your countrymen in Jamaica, are as proud of your " achievements as our fellow countrymen in " England; we join in echoing the national shouts " of gratitude and praise for the noble and

1874. Jamaica. Address of welcome.

"courageous manner in which you have in this "war aided in sustaining the glory and renoun of "the British arms.

"We feel confident that whenever the neces- "sity shall arise, you will, remembering the "victories in which you have been engaged in "Ashanti, from the gallant repulse of the enemy's "attack at Elmina to the taking of Coomassie "readily prove the loyalty and valour of British "troops to whatever part of the empire they may "belong, when engaged against foes of the British "Crown."

(Signed) K. J. KEMBLE, *Custos*, May 18, 1874.

The following Letter was received :—

Horse Guards, 28th March, 1874.

"Sir,—By desire of H.R.H. the Field "Marshal commanding-in-chief, I have the "honour to request that you will have the goodness "to publish in the General Orders of your command "the expression of the Queen's earnest thanks to "the officers and men of the 2nd West India "Regiment, for their services during the recent "operations in Western Africa, in the course of "which they have been reported by Major-General "Sir Garnet Wolseley to have been engaged in "every affair in the war, and to have undergone "fatigue and exposure in a most creditable manner, "earning thereby in common with the European "troops, Her Majesty's highest approbation.

To Officer Commanding Troops,

"West Coast of Africa.

"(Signed) W. ARMSTRONG, D.A.G.

The Regiment received the following rewards for the Ashanti campaign :—

1874. Ashanti rewards. Lieut.-Colonel Webber to be C.B.

Captains Brett, Lanyon, Turton, Haynes, and Fowler to be Brevet-Major; Lieut. Hopkins to be Captain in 16th Regiment; Lieut Jones to be Captain 96th Regiment.

The following non-commissioned officers received medals for "Distinguished Conduct in the Field" — Sergt.-Major Kelly, Coy.-Sergt.-Major Barrow, Sergeant Waison, Corporal Parris, Privates Dunn, Lewis, Fagan and Lazore. Besides this, all ranks received 30 days' pay in lieu of Batta.

On the Band leaving Demerara to join Head-quarters at Jamaica, the ladies of Georgetown presented a silver cornet to the regiment, and a handsome baton to the Bandmaster.

1874-77. Distribution. The regiment was now distributed as follows :—

Head-quarters and 3 companies at Jamaica, C.E.G.
2 companies at Barbados, H.I.
2 companies at Honduras, D.F.
2 companies at Nassau, A.B.

Issue of Ashanti medals. Medals for Ashanti Campaign were issued in July, 1875.

Nothing of interest occurred until the 30th November, 1875, when a serious fire broke out in Kingston, and the regiment was ordered out to give assistance.

1875. Jamaica. Fire in Kingston. In recognition of the services rendered, the different Insurance Companies subscribed a sum of £105, which they presented to the regiment with a suitable address.

1875.
Jamaica.
Fire in
Kingston.

The following letter was received from the Governor of Jamaica by Lieut.-Colonel Webber commanding, dated King's House, 2nd Dec., 1875.

"Sir,—I am anxious to offer to yourself, and "the officers and men of the 2nd West India Regi-"ment, the tribute of my acknowledgment of the "highly effective service which was rendered by "the regiment on Tuesday night, on the occasion "of the fire in Kingston.

"There seems to be but one opinion as to "the excellent manner in which the men of the 2nd "West India behaved in every respect; and there "can be no question that the actual assistance "they gave was of the highest value.

"All those interested in the safety of Kingston "and in the preservation of peace and good order "must feel grateful to the regiment for what they "did on Tuesday night."

I am, &c. (Signed) W. Grey.

1877.
Head-quarters
and 6
companies to
Africa.

On the 12th January, 1877, Head-quarters and six companies embarked in H.M.S. "*Simoom*," and proceeded to Sierra Leone, arriving there on the 12th February, where Head-quarters and four companies disembarked—strength—384 non-commissioned officers and men; two companies, strength 203, proceeded to Cape Coast Castle.

West Africa
and
West Indies.

On the 21st March, the "*Simoom*" having returned to Jamaica, embarked "G" company, and proceeded to Demerara, joining "H" company on the 30th, which had already removed there from Barbados, "I" company having gone temporarily to Tobago.

The regiment was now distributed as follows, 31st March, 1877.:—

1877. **Distribution.** Sierra Leone, Headquarters and B, D, E and F companies

Cape Coast Castle A and C companies

Demerara G and H companies

Tobago, I company joined the Demerara detachment at end of the year

The officers were distributed as follows :—

Africa. *Africa*—Lieut.-Colonel Webber, C.B.; Captains Matthews, Sheppard, La Touche, Stoker, Rutherford; Lieuts. Devereux, Trist, Lyster, Kerans, Hampton, Thompson, Hastings, Godwin-Austin, Norton; Sub.-Lieuts. Maunsell, Clothier, Salmon, Bauman, Dale, Dutton, Herapath; Pay-master Captain Moore, Adjutant-Lieut. Filliter.—**West Indies.** *West Indies*—Major Brett, Br.-Major Haynes; Captains Paterson, Des Barres, Talbot; Lieuts. Wilkin, Keighley, Caulfeild, Tyndale, Skelton, Sub.-Lieut. McPherson.

Col. Webber, H.P. Colonel Webber having completed five years' service as Lieut.-Colonel was placed on half-pay on 2nd February, 1878.

1878. **New Colours** On the 1st March, new Colours were issued to the regiment, and presented on parade by Colonel Webber, late commanding the regiment.

Lt.-Col. Brett appointed to command. Lieut.-Col. Brett was appointed to the command on the 2nd February, 1878, vice Colonel Webber placed on half-pay, Lieut.-Col. Turton remaining in temporary command till the 23rd January, 1879.

Issue of M.H. rifles. The Martini-Henry rifle was issued to the regiment this year.

1879. Old Colours deposited at Pro Cathedral. Demerara.

Early in July, 1879, the old Colours were sent over to the West Indies in charge of Lieut. Wainright, and on the 30th July, they were deposited in the Pro Cathedral at Georgetown, Demerara, being received by the bishop at the chancel rails with great solemnity, and in the presence of a large number of people.

West Africa.

On the 29th January, 1880, a handsome ebony baton with gold mountings was presented by "the ladies of Freetown" to the Band.

Move to West Indies.

The triennial move between the West Indies and West Africa took place this year.

The move commencing in November, 1879, was completed on 20th March, 1880, H.M.S. "*Tamar*" carried out the relief.

Distribution. 1st April, 1880.

The distribution of the regiment was as follows :—

Jamaica, Head-quarters and four companies B, D, F and G	
Nassau	one company, E
Honduras	two companies H, I
Barbados	two companies A, C

In consequence of the threatening attitude of the Ashantis at the end of 1880, it was determined by the home authorities to strengthen the garrison at Cape Coast Castle, and if necessary to undertake another expedition against them. Three companies 1st W.I. were at once moved to Cape Coast Castle from Sierra Leone, and orders were sent out to the West Indies for Head-quarters, and six companies 2nd West India to proceed to Africa at once. Accordingly Head-quarters, and B, D, F,

1881. Cape Coast. Ashanti scare. and G companies embarked at Jamaica on the hired transport "*Humber*" on the 26th February, 1881. Arriving at Barbados, A and C companies were embarked on the 3rd March, and sailing same day for Cape Coast Castle, arrived there on the 19th March.

There the regiment was scattered about the town in huts, tents and a few houses.

Colonel W. C. Justice was given command of the troops.

The quickness with which troops were brought into Cape Coast had its desired effect on King Mensa of Ashanti, and on the 4th May, the Ashanti envoys agreed to the terms, and peace was established.

The "*Humber*" being only chartered to take the regiment to Africa, sailed immediately it disembarked, so now transport had to be awaited.

On the 16th June, H.M.S. "*Orontes*" arrived with orders to take the regiment back to the West Indies. It accordingly embarked on the 18th June.

On the regiment leaving for the West Indies, Colonel Justice commanding troops, addressed the following letter to Lieut.-Col. Brett commanding 2nd West India Regiment, dated

Complimentary letter from O.C. Troops.

" H.M.S. "*Orontes*," 22nd June, 1881.

" Sir,

" Before leaving the ship, I am desirous of " communicating through you to the officers and " men of your regiment my opinion upon the state " of the regiment and the events that have " occurred during the last four months. I have no

1881. Complimentary letter from O.C. Troops.

"hesitation in saying that when the 2nd West "Indian Regiment passed into my command on "the 3rd March, 1881, no body of officers and "men could have been in a more efficient state, "and it was with great pleasure that I was able to "report to H.R.H. the Field Marshal Command-"ing-in-Chief, on the 19th March, that the con-"dition of the regiment was everything that could "be desired, and that they were fit for any duty "that could be required of them.

" Had their services been required, I feel "confident that my words would have been veri-"fied. Unfortunately the trials to which the "regiment—since their landing on the Gold Coast "—has been exposed, have been far more serious "than if they had been required to proceed on "active service.

" There can be no more severe trial to the "discipline of a regiment than when it is attacked "by epidemic disease, from which there is no "escape, and which can only be partially alleviated "by sanitary precautions and medical aid. I "have seen the test applied to your regiment "and can record to your credit, that when nearly "all the officers, European N.C. officers and a "large proportion of the West Indian N.C. officers "and men were prostrated with fever, your routine "duties were carried on, and a discipline was "maintained as accurately as if you had a blank "sick list.

" After passing through such an ordeal as "that to which your regiment has been subjected "for the last two-and-half months, you may with "honest pride return to your station in the West "Indies fully assured that the *esprit-de-corps* of "your regiment has been nobly maintained by "every man on its rolls.

1881. Complimentary letter from O.C. Troops.

" I take this opportunity of wishing you a " pleasant voyage to the West Indies and that you " may speedily regain your health.

" Should it ever be my lot to be again sent " on active service, I know no regiment I would " sooner have under my command than the '2nd " West India.' "

" I have, &c.,

" (Signed) W. C. JUSTICE, Colonel."

Casualties.

Out of the small force employed, the following casualties took place between the 1st April and the 17th June amongst the Europeans.

Died	Two officers (1st West India)
Invalided	Thirty-six officers and twelve European N.C. officers

The "*Orontes*" arriving at Barbados on the 4th July, and at Jamaica on the 16th July, the regiment resumed its former stations.

Yellow fever outbreak at Barbados.

A serious outbreak of yellow fever occurred at Barbados in the summer of 1881, attacking the 4th Regiment so severely that they were withdrawn from the island: and on the 25th October, two companies—A and G—were despatched from Jamaica to replace them.

Col. Brett placed on half pay. Col. Sir W. O. Langon appointed to command.

Colonel Brett's period of command expired on 30th October, 1882, and Colonel Sir W. O. Langon, C.B., K.C.M.G., was appointed to the command; he did not, however, assume the command, being appointed Assistant-Adjutant-General at Portsmouth on the 2nd February, 1883.

1882. Jamaica. Great Fire of Kingston, Dec. 11th, 1882.

The greatest fire which ever occurred in Kingston took place on the 11th December, 1882, a big block of streets (including Harbour Street) of about a mile long by half-a-mile deep was utterly destroyed—this was the business part of the city, and included the ordnance store.

General Gamble, C.B., who was actually inspecting the regiment at the time, ordered it out at once. The fire lasted the whole night, and the regiment gave valuable assistance in preventing it from spreading, and also in keeping order.

The following letter from the Governor of Jamaica, dated 12th December, was addressed to Major-General Gamble, commanding troops:

"Sir,

" On behalf of the government of this
" colony no less than on that of the inhabitants of
" Kingston, I ask you to accept my thanks for the
" willing and valuable assistance rendered to the
" townspeople by Colonel Wiseman-Clarke and the
" officers and men of the garrison at Up Park
" Camp, acting under your Excellency's command
" during the occurrence of the calamitous fire of
" yesterday, and I beg your Excellency to convey
" to Colonel Wiseman-Clarke and the officers and
" men of the garrison my high appreciation of the
" important character of their services, and the
" good conduct so conspicuously displayed by the
" troops.

" I have, &c., &c.,

" (Signed) A. MUSGRAVE."

This letter Major-General Gamble published in local General Orders, fully endorsing the Governor's remarks.

1883.
Wreck of s.s. "Bolivar."

In January, 1883, the War Office decided to make a further change in the garrisoning of the West Coast of Africa, and directed that on the triennial relief, then about to take place, that (3) three companies 2nd West India were to relieve the Head-quarters and six companies 1st West India, then on the coast, and the hired transport "*Bolivar*" was despatched from England to carry out this service.

That vessel, however, was wrecked on the Coblers rock, Barbados; Major Talbot commanding troops on board: all the baggage was lost, but no lives. H.M.S. "*Tyne*" was then detailed for this duty, commencing in Africa.

1883.
Lt.-Col. Sheppard appointed to command.

Lieut.-Colonel Sheppard was appointed to command *vice* Colonel Sir W. Lanyon, employed on the Staff, on 2nd February, 1883.

Head-quarters move to Barbados.
Detachment 3 companies to W.C. Africa.

On the 9th March, Head-quarters and C, D and F companies embarked in H.M.S. "*Tyne*" for Barbados, arriving there on the 15th, and on the 16th the detachment of three companies—A, C and F—sailed for West Africa, disembarking F company at Cape Coast Castle, on the 1st April, and A and C companies at Sierra Leone on the 6th April.

The following officers accompanied the detachment to Africa—Major Talbot (to command at Sierra Leone); Captains Tyndale (to command at Cape Coast Castle), Skelton; Lieuts. Wainright, Northcott, Brooker, Hackett and Tottenham, the three latter for Cape Coast Castle.

Head-quarters move to Africa.

Early in May, in consequence of threatened complications with Ashanti, the Governor of the Gold Coast protested against the proposed reduction of the African garrisons; it was decided,

1883. Head-quarters move to Africa.

after all, that the Head-quarters and three more companies should go over, and, consequently, telegraphic orders were received to that effect, and on the "*Tyne*" arriving at Barbados with the two companies H and I, from Honduras, Head-quarters and D company embarked on the 31st May for Africa.

The following officers accompanied Head-quarters—Lt.-Colonel Sheppard, Major Caulfeild, Lieuts. Ogilby, Lysaght (Adjutant), Townsend, Coleman, and Qr.-Mr. Kelly; B, E and G companies being left at Barbados.

West Africa. Sherbro Expedition.

Before the Head-quarters arrived at Sierra Leone, the detachment there was engaged on service as follows:—

In consequence of disturbances between the natives of the Hinterland and the people of Sherbro, a force consisting of three subalterns (Lieuts. Northcott, Paterson, and Barton) and 60 non-commissioned officers and men, under command of Captain Skelton, were despatched from Sierra Leone in the colonial steamer "*Prince of Wales*" on the 18th May, followed by another party on the 22nd May, consisting of Lieut.-Colonel Talbot, Lieuts. Dunn and McFarlane, 60 non-commissioned officers and men, and two howitzers.

The force under Captain Skelton had, in the meantime, on the 21st May, attacked and destroyed the town Momallikee.

On the 23rd, the whole force, under command of Lieut.-Colonel Talbot, accompanied by 80 police, left Bomthe for Talliah, the principal stronghold of Epowe, the chief of the hostile tribes.

1883. West African Sherbro Expedition.

The towns of Cortemahoo and Hahoo were attacked in succession, the former being burned. The force stopped at Hahoo that night, and next morning—24th—marched to Talliah, two miles distant; this town was taken and destroyed, after about two hours' resistance, with a loss of only two men wounded.

The party then returned to Bomthe, destroying Hahoo *en route*.

On the 25th, half the force returned to Freetown, leaving Captain Skelton and one subaltern and 70 men at Bomthe till the 9th June, when they embarked and arrived at Freetown on the 10th.

The following Letters were received in acknowledgment of the service :—

Letter from Horse Guards.

" Horse Guards, 29th June, 1883.

" Sir,

" I have the honour, by desire of the Field " Marshal Commanding-in-Chief, to acknowledge " receipt of your letter of the 29th ultimo, " forwarding a copy of the communication from " the Administrator-in-Chief, West African " Settlement, relative to the recent expedition " against Talliah, testifying to the excellent service " rendered by the troops under your command on " that occasion.

" In reply I have it in command to acquaint " you, that this testimony to the zeal and conduct " of the men in the field under such trying " circumstances has afforded his Royal Highness " much satisfaction.

" I have, &c., &c.,

" (Signed) Geo. Harman, D.A.G."

1883. Letter from War Office.

" War Office, 9th July, 1883.

" Sir,

" I am directed by the Secretary of State to " acknowledge receipt of your despatch of 29th " May last, giving detailed account of the recent " military expedition to Sherbro, and its successful " termination.

" In reply, I am to express to you the " satisfaction with which H.R.H. the Field Marshal " Commanding-in-Chief and the Secretary of " State have received your testimony to the " conduct of the several officers and men who were " employed under your orders.

" Lord Hartington desires me further to " convey to you his approval of your proceedings " in the conduct of the expedition.

" I have, &c., &c.,

" (Signed) Ralph Thompson.

" To Lt.-Col. Talbot,

" Commanding Troops, W. C. Africa."

Letter from Col. Office.

In a letter from the Secretary of State for the Colonies to the Governor of West African Settlements, dated 6th November, 1883, is the following paragraph:—" I have informed the " Secretary of State for War that, in my opinion, " Colonel Talbot's management of the military " portion of the affair has been very creditable to " him, and that the success of the expedition was " largely due to his skilful and effective " arangements."

Nothing of interest occurred during the remainder of this tour of service on the coast.

Chapter XV.

1885. Move from Africa to West Indies.

The triennial relief commenced by three companies embarking at Sierra Leone on the 23rd September, 1885, in H.M.S. "*Tyne*," A and F companies disembarking at Belize on the 19th October, and C company at Nassau on the 15th October.

Head-quarters and three companies embarked at Sierra Leone on the 17th February, having been detained a month on account of the unsettled state of the Sierra Leone Hinterland.

The three companies, B, E, and G, having, previously to the "*Tyne*" going over to Africa, moved from Barbados to Jamaica in November.

Head-quarters arrived at Jamaica from Sierra Leone on the 10th March, 1886.

1886. Distribution of Regiment West Indies.

The distribution of the regiment was:—

Jamaica, Head-quarters and B, D, E, G, H, and I Companies.

Honduras A and F Companies

Nassau C Company

The regiment was inspected by Major-General Pearson, both Head-quarters and the detachments, in March, 1886.

1887. Col. Sheppard to H.P. Lt.-Col. Talbot appointed to command, 2nd Feb., 1887.

Colonel Sheppard having completed his period of command, was placed on half-pay on the 2nd February, 1887, and Lieut.-Col. Talbot was appointed to the command on the same day.

Concentration of troops in West Indies.

It was now decided to withdraw gradually all the troops from the out-lying West Indian Colonies, and to concentrate them at the places which were to be strongly fortified and made into coaling stations in accordance with the Imperial Defence Scheme. Jamaica and St. Lucia were selected, and in pursuance of this arrangement, one company (F), was ordered to Jamaica from Honduras, arriving there on the 24th February, 1887, this made seven companies at Jamaica, five being stationed at Up Park Camp, one at Port Royal, and one at Apostle's Battery, at the mouth of the harbour.

Queen's Jubilee.

On the 28th June, 1887, all the available officers attended a State service at the Parish Church, Kingston, which was held in celebration of Her Majesty's Jubilee.

In the afternoon, a brigade consisting of the troops, Militia, and naval contingent from the ships of war, paraded in review order, at Up Park

1887. West Indies. Queen's Jubilee

Camp, the Governor, Sir Henry Norman, being present, Colonel Justice commanding the brigade, Colonel Talbot being in command of the battalion. The regimental Colour was trooped, after which the brigade marched past.

Colonel Talbot retires, Lt.-Patchett appointed to command.

Colonel Talbot retired with the honorary rank of Major-General on the 29th June, 1887, and Lieut.-Col. Patchett was appointed to the command on the same date.

1888. Withdrawal from Honduras.

On the 5th May, the troops were finally withdrawn from Honduras, and letter "A" company arrived at Jamaica from that place on the 9th May, 1888.

The whole regiment with the exception of "C" company was now stationed at Jamaica. Six companies at Up Park Camp, one company at Port Royal, and one company at Apostle's Battery.

Amalgamation of 1st and 2nd W.I., 1st October, 1888.

Early in the year, intimation was received that the two West India regiments would be amalgamated on the 1st October.

The new regiment to be called "The West India Regiment," to be composed of two battalions of eight companies each, and a depot formed out of the ninth company of each regiment, also that as soon as sufficient barrack accommodation could be provided, one whole battalion would in future be stationed on the West Coast. The regiment to be composed of one colonel, five lieutenant-colonels (one to command depôt), six majors, fifteen captains, thirty-six lieutenants, eighteen 2nd lieutenants, two adjutants, three quarter-masters.

The facings and tassels to be white, except band and drummers, who were to have yellow tassels.

1888. West Indies. The facings and tassels of the 2nd West India were consequently changed from yellow to white.

On the 29th September, the regiment paraded as strong as possible, and the regimental colour of the 2nd West India Regiment was trooped for the last time, before becoming the 2nd battalion West India Regiment.

Move to Africa. On the 2nd November, 1888, the triennial relief of the West African Garrisons commenced, and was completed on the 18th March, 1889, H.M.S. "*Tyne*" performing the service.

Distribution of the Battalion. The battalion was now distributed as follows :—

Sierra Leone.—Head-quarters and C, D, E, F, G, companies, the officers being Lieut.-Col. Patchett; Majors Foster and Howarth; Captains McPherson, Bayley, Barton, Dunn, Hatch; Lieuts. Tottenham, Drake, Morgan, McFall, Lees (Adjutant), Brooks, Bristow, Henstock, Kenna; 2nd Lieuts. Luard, Boddam, Lendy, Baker, Slessor. Loveband, Cloran; Lieut. and Quartermaster Crane.

Cape Coast Castle.—"A" and "B" companies, officers being Major Bingham; Captains Claridge and Turner; Lieuts. Buck, Dalrymple-Hay, Oates, and De Cerjat.

Demerara.—"H" company and the following officers, Major Caulfeild; Lieuts. Jackson, Walter, Sherwood, and Blackden.

A small detachment was stationed at Robarri, sixty miles inland from Freetown, Lieut. Lendy being in command.

1890. **West Africa.** On the 25th February, 1890, Lieut. Lendy was given a D.S.O. for operations against the slave traders at Foulah Town.

1891. **Withdrawal from Cape Coast.** On the 25th February, 1891, the detachment at Cape Coast Castle, consisting of "A" and "B" companies was withdrawn to Sierra Leone, making seven companies at headquarters.

On the 19th March, 1891, the detachment at Robarri was withdrawn.

Withdrawal from Demerara, May. On the 7th May, 1891, the detachment at Demerara was moved to St. Lucia, the troops being withdrawn finally from the former station.

Lt.-Col. Patchett to Half-Pay. Lt.-Col. Maltby appointed to command. On the 22th June, 1891, Lieut.-Col. Patchett, having completed four years in command, was placed on half-pay, and Lieut.-Col. Maltby was appointed to command on the same date.

Detachment to Gambia. In consequence of an uneasy feeling with regard to the native tribes at the Gambia, it was decided to sent a small detachment there from Sierra Leone, and on the 11th July, 1891, two officers and fifty N.C.O.'s and men of "E" company embarked at Freetown in s.s. "*Coanza*" for Bathurst.

Fodey Cabba, an important chief near the Gambia settlement, had been giving trouble to the traders for some time past, causing considerable stagnation in the trade of the settlement.

It was decided to send a small joint naval military force against him to bring him to his senses.

1892. Gambia Expedition against Fodey Cabba.

On the 29th December, 1891, a force composed of Major Claridge in command, Lieuts. Lees, Carleton, Rew; Regtl. Sergt.-Major Colley, and 120 N.C. officers and men embarked at Freetown on H.M.S. "*Racer*," "*Thrush*" and "*Widgeon*" for conveyance to Bathurst, the force was augmented on arrival by Captain Bayley, Lieut. Drake, and 50 N.C. officers and men already stationed there. The naval contingent consisted of Commander Royle, H.M.S. "*Racer*," in command of the expedition; Lieut.-Commander Loane, R.N., and 17 bluejackets.

On the 2nd January, 1892, a party consisting of five officers and 102 N.C. officers and men 2nd West India Regiment and 17 bluejackets, the whole under command of Lieut.-Commander Loane, affected a landing at Kinsala on the south side of Vintang Creek.

On the 3rd January, they captured Sangajor and returned to Bathurst.

On the 14th, a party consisting of three officers and 65 N.C. officers and men, with one officer and 23 men Gambia Police, proceeded to Kinsala.

On the 17th, they took and burnt Jibbok after a slight resistance, Kibok and Kawali, and returned to Kaling, having marched 25 miles that day.

The enemy, about 300 strong, attacked Kaling on the morning of the 19th; they were armed with flint-lock trade guns and a few rifles, and advanced to within 400 yards of the camp. Fire was opened on them and they retired in 15 minutes followed up by Lieut. Lees and 30 men, who could not follow them far owing to the thickness of the bush.

1892. Gambia Expedition against Fodey Cabba.

On the 23rd Lieut.-Commander Frazer who was in command of this part of the force, ordered a parade of all the troops and complimented the men of the battalion on the excellent way they marched and performed their duties.

Major Claridge was invalided to the "*Racer*" and Captain Bayley assumed command of the West India detachment.

It was arranged that Moussa Molloh and his men, chiefly mounted, should unite with the Expeditionary Force on the 3rd February in front of Kusumbu, a town under the influence of Fodey Cabba, but it was discovered that he had left the place, so that plan was abandoned, and in consequence the force returned to Bathurst on the 5th February.

The detachment of the battalion embarked for West Indies on the 23rd February on board the transport s.s. "*Atlas*," being relieved by a detachment of the 1st Battalion.

War Medals granted.

For this service the West African Medal was issued to all engaged, and No. 3171 Corporal E. Forde was promoted sergeant for capturing five of the enemy while crossing the Vintang Creek, at Kinsala.

Battalion to West Indies.

The triennial relief commenced on the 5th January, the Head-quarters moving first, transport s.s. "*Atlas*" performing this duty, which was completed on the 16th March.

The battalion was now distributed as follows:—

Jamaica, Head-quarters, and A, D, E and H companies

Barbados, F and G companies

St. Lucia, B and C companies

1892.
Lt.-Col. Maltby retires, Lt.-Col. Caulfeild to command, 24th February, 1892.

On the 24th February Lieut.-Col. Maltby retired on a pension, and Lieut.-Col. Caulfeild was appointed to the command.

General's Inspection.

The battalion was inspected by Major-General Black, C.B., on the 26th June, 1892, and the remarks of H.R.H. the Commander-in-Chief, were that he " considered it a generally satisfactory report."

1893.
General's Inspection.

The battalion was again inspected by Major-General Black, on 26th January, 1893. H.R.H. the Commander-in-Chief's remarks were that he " considered it a satisfactory report."

Old Colours at Demerara.

The old Colours of the regiment, which were presented by H.R.H. the Duke of Edinburgh, on the 4th December, 1861, and laid up in the Pro Cathedral, Demerara, on the 30th July, 1879, were removed with military honours and due solemnity from the Pro Cathedral to the new Cathedral, on the 13th April.

The Colours were handed by the Revd. Canon Castell to Lieut. Anson and 2nd Lieut. Swain, of the British Guiana Militia, with the usual colour escort of sergeants, and received at the door of the Pro Cathedral by a Militia Guard of Honour, and carried to the new Cathedral, where, in the presence of a large assembly, they were placed on the alter, after which a sermon was preached by the Revd. P. A. Stevenson, in which he referred to the depositing of the Colours in the Pro Cathedral in 1879, on which occasion His Lordship, the late Bishop Austin, conducted the service.

Battalion join Army Rifle Association.

The battalion joined the Army Rifle Association this year, and competed for the following events :—

1893. Battalion join Army Rifle Association.

Queen's Cup, taking 53rd place; Young Soldiers' Cup, taking 18th place; Inter Company Volley, E Company being 54th, D Company 76th, A Company 85th, and H Company 87th on the list.

Issue of Medals for Gambia.

Medals for the Gambia Expedition of 1892 were presented to the officers and men engaged, on the 21st April, 1893, at a Brigade parade, by Lady Blake, the wife of the Governor of Jamaica. The following officers received medals: Major Claridge, Captain Bayley, Lieuts. Drake, Lees, Carleton, 2nd Lieut. Rew, and 176 warrant non-commissioned officers and men.

1894. General's Inspection.

The battalion was inspected on the 12th February, 1894, by Major-General Bengough, C.B., who on completion of the Inspection, addressed the battalion as follows:—

"Colonel Caulfeild, officers, and non-com-
"missioned officers and men of the 2nd Battalion
"West India Regiment, when last I inspected
"you, I told you I had heard very favourable
"reports of you, of your soldierly bearing and
"conduct, and that you did your work well.

"Since then I have seen you many times,
"and the favourable opinion previously formed, I
"am now pleased to tell you, on this, my second
"inspection of you this morning, has been con-
"firmed. It shows that the training of Colonel
"Caulfeild and the officers, has been of the best,
"and diligently carried out.

"Your bayonet exercise and physical drill
"could not have been better, we are not any of
"us perfect, and I would point out that there was a
"little too much noise from the supernumerary
"rank during battalion drill, but on the whole I
"am very well pleased with everything I saw.

1894. Jamaica. General's Inspection.

"I have seen many regiments, and in "manœuvre and general working, I consider you "are second to none. You need not fear com- "parison with any other troops, for any emergency "in which you may be called upon to act. . . . "Colonel Caulfeild I shall have much pleasure in "making a very favourable report of your battalion "to H.R.H. the Commander-in-Chief."

H.R.H. Commander-in-Chief's remarks

His Royal Highness the Commander-in-Chief's remarks on this Inspection Report were, that he "considered it satisfactory and creditable "to all concerned."

Marching Competition.

A marching competition took place on the 14th February under the following conditions :—

Each company to start at the following strength, viz. :—1 officer and 80 N.C. officers and men, 800 being the highest possible score; drill order. The object being to bring the largest number of men into action by firing a volley at end of the march, distance nine miles; two compulsory halts of not less than three minutes during the march, and no doubling allowed.

The penalties were: ten (10) points to be deducted for every man falling out, five points for every man not firing in the volley, and twenty points deducted per minute of company behind the quickest company.

The results was as follows :—

"D"	company	1hr.	55 mins.	Total points	755
"H"	,,	1 ,,	59½ ,,	,,	690
"A"	,,	2 ,,	1¾ ,,	,,	640
"E"	,,	2 ,,	4¾ ,,	,,	585

1894. Jamaica.

The following Brigade Order was published:

"The Major-General commanding desires "to compliment the 2nd West India Regiment on "the manner in which a company contest in "marching was carried out yesterday morning, "such exercises when carried through in a practical "and soldier-like manner are of great military value, "affording a test of what soldiers can accomplish "in the all important direction of rapid marching."

The battalion again entered this year for the following competitions in the Army Rifle Association:

Queen's Cup—taking 62nd place.

Young Soldiers' Cup—taking 53rd place.

Inter-Company Volley—"D" taking 63rd place.

Fracas with the Police.

On the 8th June, a fracas occurred between some soldiers and police which led to very unpleasant consequences.

It appears that a few days previously a policeman, taking advantage of his position as such, attempted to arrest a man of "A" company with whom he had had some high words about a woman. Some men, also belonging to "A" company, standing near by, seeing that their comrade was being, as they considered, unfairly dealt with, unfortunately took the law into their own hands, and attempted to rescue him, with the result that several were arrested and brought up next day before the magistrate, and punished for interfering with the police; this made a hostile feeling amongst the men of "A" company towards the police, and early the following evening they began to use threats against the police, and later on, having collected a body of about 50 men,

1894. Fracas with the Police.

partly belonging to the battalion and partly to the depôt, under the leadership of Lance-Corporal Phillips, they proceeded to Sutton Street and Fletcher's Land police stations, and smashed the windows with stones. While on their way from one station to another they twice came into contact with the police picquets. During these melées, an inspector and two constables were wounded by being cut with a razor; this is supposed to have been done by Phillips.

Immediately the news was received at camp, picquets were sent out, and the whole affair was over within two hours.

Unfortunately the local press were only too glad to exaggerate the disturbance into a general mutiny of the native troops.

It was a most unfortunate and regrettable affair, but considering that only 50 men, as estimated by the police, out of nearly 1000 native troops in camp took part in it, and that the picquets sent out after the rioters did their work right well, no one but an alarmist, or most unfriendly to the regiment, could consider that it was anything else than a street row, got up without premeditation, and absolutely confined to the few who took part in it. However the local military authorities did not take such a view of it, and the battalion was looked upon as if it were either on the verge of, or had already mutinied. Then began systematic hustling of the battalion in such a manner, that if the discipline had not been excellent, serious consequences might have arisen.

During this trying time there was an absolute absence of crime, the men taking their punishment, as it really was, cheerfully and without the least sign of discontent or insubordination.

1894. Jamaica.

Unfortunately the governor, Sir Henry Blake, was absent on leave from May till November, but immediately on his return, brighter times came for the regiment.

The General Officer commanding left for England immediately on the Governor's return.

The latter at once requested the Officer commanding troops to take off all the restrictions and precautions imposed by the General Officer commanding, feeling as he did, that the battalion had been a victim to public ill-feeling and alarmists; he at once granted a free pardon to Lance-Corporal Latibeaudier, who had been wrongfully convicted, this being done at the instance of the Judge and Inspector-general of Police. Although sentence had been passed in accordance with the finding of the jury, judgment had been stayed pending the case being laid before the Governor on his return.

Issue of Lee-Metford Rifle.

The Lee-Metford rifle was issued to the battalion in August, 1894.

On the 12th December, at the request of the Governor, the battalion and depôt were paraded, and he addressed them as follows:—

Governor's Address.

"Colonel Caulfeild, officers and men of the "West India Regiment, I have come to-day to "parade the regiment and to say farewell before "you sail for the West Coast, as in all human pro-"bability, this may be the last time we shall ever "meet. I have known the regiment off and on for "over ten years in Nassau and in Jamaica; and, in "my experience, the regiment has been faithful "and true, shewing soldierly qualities of discipline "at home, as it has given evidence on the West "Coast of its valour in the face of the enemy. I

1894.
Governor's Address.

"have twice been present on parade for the presentation of medals, for the Yonnie and the "Gambia Expeditions, and I see before me some "of you who bear upon your breasts the proud token "that you have served your Queen and country in "the field.

" I was sorry to hear that during my absence "there had been some trouble in June last. I "have looked over all the papers since I came "back, and regret that a few foolish, hot-tempered "men should have allowed themselves to forget "that if a soldier is to retain the friendship of the "people, and the respect due to the wearer of Her "Majesty's uniform, he must reserve his fighting "for the enemies of his country. I am certain "that the old soldiers of the depot and battalion "regret this occurrence as much as I do, and I "will go further and say that I am sure that the men "who were engaged in this business regret it also.

" I look upon the riot of the 8th of June as "the foolish outbreak of a few men, for I am "certain that the numbers mentioned as having "been there were greatly exaggerated, and I see "no reason to change the opinion I have always "held of the soldierly qualities of the regiment. "You will understand that when a number of "letters are received saying that there is to be an "attack by the regiment upon the people of "Kingston or upon the police before you sail, the "responsibilities of disregarding those letters are "very great; but I think that those letters have "come from very nervous people. I do not believe "those fears well founded, for the conduct of the "regiment from that day to the present has been "admirable, and I do not believe that there is any "intention on the part of the regiment to mis-"conduct themselves in any way. I have therefore, "asked Colonel Spencer to cancel that Order

1894. The Governor's farewell address.

"placing Kingston out of bounds, for I feel that "men who are leaving the island on foreign service "should have an opportunity of saying good-bye "to their friends. The best proof that my "confidence has not been misplaced is that last "night there was not a single man absent from roll "call, a circumstance of which any regiment "might well be proud.

" I am glad once more to see this fine "regiment on parade, I wish you every good "fortune in the future and I am certain that if "occasion arises of active service in Africa, you "will shew the same valiant and soldier-like "qualities in the future that you have always dis-"played in the past."

In order that his opinion should be known to the public, His Excellency had the above address sent to all the principal papers in Kingston for publication.

R.H.S. Medal to Lieut. Hardyman.

Three days previously, 12th December, a silver medal granted by the Royal Humane Society, was presented on parade by Mrs. Caulfeild, wife of the officer commanding, to Lieut. W. H. Hardyman, for "assisting to save two girls who had been "surrounded by the tide at Plimont, Jersey, on the "29th September, 1894."

Move to Africa.

On the 16th December, the triennial change between West Indies and West Africa commenced, by two companies embarking on the hired transport "*Warwick Castle*," under command of Major Dunn, proceeding to Barbados, there embarking the detachment, and from thence to Sierra Leone.

1894. Honduras. On the 17th, Orders were received to hold a detachment of 120 men in readiness to embark for Belize in aid of civil power, and on the following day, 18th, a detachment consisting of Major Bayley, Captain Blackden, Lieuts. Carleton, Murison and Magan, and 120 non-commissioned officers and men of "H" company embarked in s.s. "*City of Kingston*" and sailed for Belize.

On arrival there, they found the town in a state of excitement almost verging on panic; however, the unexpectedly quick arrival of troops made matters quiet down. Although they had not to be actually employed in quelling disturbance, the duty of guarding the town against the threatening rioters was very severe.

1895. The "*Warwick Castle*" arrived from Africa picking up "B" and "C" companies *en route* at St. Lucia, landed them at Jamaica on the 24th January, and proceeded at once to Belize to relieve the detachment by a similar detachment of the 1st battalion and arrived back at Jamaica on the 1st February.

Head-quarters embark for Africa. On the 7th February, Head-quarters and B, C, D and H companies embarked for Africa, and arrived at Sierra Leone on the 24th February.

The whole eight (8) companies of the battalion were now together, the first time for many years.

Centenary of Battalion, 24th April, 1895. The battalion reached its centenary on the 24th April, 1895.

On which date the following were serving with it:—

1895. Strength of Battalion. Africa.

Lieut.-Col.	J. E. Caulfeild,—Commanding	
,,	G. Madden, C.B., D.S.O.,	(on leave)
Major	A. L. Bayley	(depot)
,,	C. Dunn	
,,	R. Egerton	
,,	T. P. Lowry	
,,	H. C. Buck	(on leave)
Captain	J. Dalrymple-Hay	(adjt.-volunteers)
,,	R. B. Todd	(Staff-Off. Militia)
,,	C. W. Young	(depot)
,,	W. L. Jackson	
,,	W. B. Stansfeld	(on leave)
,,	F. E. Ryde	(on leave)
,,	O. C. Sherwood	(adjt. O.S. Dept.)
,,	C. B. Morgan	(Niger Coy.)
,,	L. A. Brooks	(O.S. Dept)
,,	F. T. Henstock	(adjutant)
,,	F. R. Loveband	(staff)
,,	A. W. Wilson	
,,	E. Baines	(on leave)
,,	V. C. Climo	(on leave)
Lieutenant	F. A. Liston	(depot)
,,	E. A. Barchard	(on leave)
,,	H. D. Carleton	(depot, staff)
,,	F. R. Barton	(staff)
,,	W. K. Falcon	

1895. Strength of Battalion.

Lieutenant		J. P. Alone	
	,,	J. S. Henderson	
	,,	W. H. Hardyman	
	,,	C. E. D. O. Rew	(depot)
	,,	J. E. Woodman	(Hythe)
	,,	R. Litchford	
	,,	B. H. Drury	(garr.-adjt.)
	,,	T. B. Fulton	
	,,	H. A. Thorne	
	,,	F. Lynch Blosse	
	,,	J. P. Bliss	
	,,	E. Saunders-Davies	
	,,	D. Poole	(on leave)
	,,	W. W. Davis	(on leave)
	,,	A. T. Martin	
	,,	S. E. Beamish	
	,,	G. Peacocke	
	,,	A. T. Magan	
2nd	,,	W. Chill	
	,,	A. B. Murison	
	,,	P. E. Prideaux	
	,,	C. P. Greig	(not joined)
	,,	G. E. Hewitt	do.
	,,	F. Swaby	do.
Lt.&Qr.-Mr.		E. Crane	

2 Warrant officers, Sergt.-Maj. Wallace and B. M. Gornell

1895. Strength of Battalion.

4 staff sergeants
13 company sergeant-majors
32 sergeants
16 drummers
844 corporals and privates

(End of First Hundred Years).

Chapter XVI.

1895. Ashanti Expedition to Kumassi.

The Home authorities having decided to annex Ashanti, an expedition to Kumassi was undertaken, and in conjunction with the 2nd Battalion East Yorkshire Regiment and a special service battalion composed of drafts from 20 European Regiments; a Wing consisting of E, F, G and H companies was ordered to take part. The following were the officers:—

Major A. L. Bayley in command of Wing, Major T. P. E. Lowry; Captains F. T. Henstock, A. W. Wilson, V. C. Climo, F. A. Liston, N. P. Davies; Lieuts. W. H. Hardyman, J. E. S. Woodman, B. H. Drury, H. A. Thorne, F. L. Blosse, J. P. Bliss, E. L. S. Davies, D. Poole, A. T. de M. Martin, S. E. Beamish, A. T. Magan, A. B. Murison; 2nd Lieut. P. E. Prideaux.

The Wing embarked at Sierra Leone on the 14th December, 1895, in s.s. "*Loanda*," arrived at Cape Coast Castle on the 18th, and marched up country on the 20th December, leaving "H" company at the base.

1896. **Ashanti Expedition to Kumassi.**

Kumassi was occupied on the 18th January, 1896, without any resistance, the King (Prempeh) made prisoner, and the expedition returned to Cape Coast Castle, leaving a garrison of Gold Coast Houssas at Kumassi.

The Wing returned to Head-quarters on the 9th March, 1896.

Rewards.

The following rewards were granted for this service. Major Bayley to be Brevet Lt.-Colonel, and the Ashanti star to all ranks.

1897. **Benin Expedition Akassa.**

In consequence of the naval expedition to Benin, the Niger Houssas being required to take part, it was decided to occupy Akassa with troops in order to prevent a disturbance between the natives of that place and the Brass people. A company composed of half "A" and half "B" with the following officers embarked on the 26th January, 1897:

Major Dalrymple-Hay in command, Captain Stansfeld, Lieuts. R. Litchford and A. Martin. On the successful termination of the expedition, the detachment returned to Head-quarters, Sierra Leone, on the 20th April, 1897.

Annual Inspection.

On the 17th March, 1897, the battalion was inspected at Sierra Leone, by Colonel Caulfeild, commanding troops West Coast of Africa, with the following result:—

Commander-in-Chief remarks, dated 19th October, 1897, "he considers it a satisfactory "Report."

Gold Coast and Lagos Hinterlands.

In consequence of French aggression in the Hinterland of the Gold Coast and Lagos, it was decided to occupy effectively the whole of these Hinterlands claimed by Great Britain, a conference sitting at Paris deciding the validity of the British and French claims.

1897. On the 6th May, 1897, "C" and "E" companies embarked for Cape Coast Castle, with the following officers :—

Lieut.-Col. D. M. Allen in command; Capt. N. P. Davies; Lieuts. W. H. Hardyman, S. E. Beamish, W. Chill and 2nd Lieut. A. S. Durnford. This detachment was stationed at Cape Coast Castle until the 30th September, when "C" company was ordered to Lagos, joining "F" and "G" companies, which embarked at Sierra Leone, on the 26th September, 1897.

2nd Lieut. Durnford died on the 24th May.

The following officers proceeded to Lagos, from Head-quarters :—

Major Dalrymple-Hay; Lieuts. F. L. Blosse, A. Murison, P. Prideaux; 2nd Lieuts. F. Swaby and E. Marindin.

From Cape Coast Castle :—

Lieut. Colonel D. Allen in command; Lieuts. Hardyman and Bliss.

Two companies "F" and "G" proceeded to Saki, leaving Lagos on the 26th October, 1897, and arriving at Saki on the 15th November, a distance of 250 miles.

In consequence of the unsettled state of affairs on the West Coast of Africa, the Order for the embarkation of the Head-quarters in s.s. "*Spartan*" on the 10th December, 1897, was cancelled by telegram from the War Office on the 5th December.

1898. Distribution of the Battalion. The distribution of the battalion on the 1st January, 1898, was as follows:—

Head-quarters and A, B, D & H companies Sierra Leone. C, F, G companies, Lagos; and E company, Cape Coast Castle.

On the 21st January, 1898, letter "E" company under command of Major C. W. Young, was ordered to proceed to Kumassi, and "B" company was ordered to proceed there also from Sierra Leone, embarking on the 27th January.

The following officers accompanied "B" company:—Captain A. E. Barchard; Lieuts. C. E. D. O. Rew and H. A. Thorne.

Head-quarters and letters A, D and H companies, under command of Brevet Lieut.-Col. Bayley were ordered by cablegram from the War Office, to proceed on the 5th February to Lagos.

Colonel Caulfeild to half-pay. Lt.-Col. Allen to command. Colonel Caulfeild having completed his extended period of command was placed on half-pay on the 24th February, Lieut.-Colonel D. M. Allen, succeeding to the command.

CHRONOLOGICAL EVENTS.

1795	Regiment raised at St. Vincent, Lieut.-Colonel Graham in command Move to Martinique Move to St. Vincent
1796	Carib War, Actions of Calonery, Vegie, &c.
1797	Lieut.-Colonel Carmichael in command Move to Grenada False alarm at Grenada
1798	Volunteers to subscribe towards expenses of French war
1799	First inspection
1800	First Colours Embarks for Trinidad Loss of the "*Dromedary*"
1801	Expedition against Danish West Indies Taking of St. Bartholemey, St. Martin, &c. Move to Jamaica
1802	Embarkation and disembarkation at Jamaica
1803	Martial Law enforced at Jamaica
1804	Two companies sent for service to Bahamas Establishment raised to 1,000
1805	French threaten Jamaica Thanks received from Commander-in-Chief
1807	Two companies returned from Bahamas "Gunners" first formed in regiment
1808	Mutiny of recruits Five non-commissioned officers and men decorated for gallantry

1809	Attack on St. Domingo Move to Bahamas
1814	American war, storming of Fort Petrie
1816	New Colours Move to Jamaica
1818	Five companies to Honduras
1819	Head-quarters and five companies to West Africa Two companies to Bahamas Destruction of Barracks at Isle de Los Severe loss from climate
1820	Rio Pongo Expedition, capture of Curtistown
1823	Ashanti war, Actions of Dunquah Essecumah
1824	Ashanti War, action and defeat at Assamacow, death of Sir C. McCarthy Action at Beulah, defence of Cape Coast Defeat of Ashantis
1825	Head-quarters return to West Indies (Bahamas) Loss of records and books Recruiting company formed at Sierra Leone
1826	Sherbro Expedition
1827	Inspection at Nassau
1828	Inspection at Nassau under command of Lieut.-Colonel MacDonald
1830	New Colours presented, old ones burnt Head-quarters to Honduras
1831	Capture of Fort Bullen
1832	Head-quarters to Bahamas
1835	Lieut.-Colonel Patterson died
1838	Fire at Belize
1839	Head-quarters to Jamaica (Spanishtown)
1841	Head-quarters to Jamaica (Up Park Camp)

1842	Called out in aid of civil power Sir William Gomm's message Third West India Regiment raised
1843	Two companies to Gambia Fire at Kingston (Jamaica)
1844	Lieut.-Colonel Nicholls died
1845	Head-quarters moved to Nassau Lieut.-Colonel Cobbe takes over command
1846	Two companies join Head-quarters from Jamaica
1847	New colours presented at Nassau Two companies moved from Jamaica to Trinidad and St. Lucia
1848	Head-quarters move from Nassau to Jamaica Regiment called out in aid of civil power Change of companies at Gambia
1849	Nos. 2 and 5 Companies move from Honduras to Grenada and Tobago Keeming Expedition Storming of Bambucko Cage Coote Expedition
1851	Moves in West Indies, Head-quarters to Demerara
1852	Moves in West Indies
1853	Change of companies in Africa Storming of Sabbagee
1854	Fire at Belize Relief of Christiansborg First Malageah Expedition
1855	Second Malageah Expedition Second Sabbagee Expedition Storming of Sabbagee Regiment volunteers for Crimea

1856 Reinforcements for Africa
Riots in British Guiana (called out)
Inspection by Sir A. Cloete
New accoutrements received

1857 Move of companies from Africa to West Indies
Head-quarters move from Demerara to Jamaica
Enfield rifle received
Establishment raised to 1,295
Inspection by Major-General Bell

1858 Detachment to Honduras
Establishment reduced to ordinary
Zouave uniform received

1859 Called out in aid of civil power (Jamaica)

1860 Inspected by Major-General Taylor
Six companies to Africa
Wreck of the "*Perseverance*"

1861 Baddiboo War
Abbeokuta disturbance
Quiah War
Action of Kabaie
Attack of Massago
Storming of Madonkia
Defence of Songotown
Action at Madonkia
Action at Robea
Head-quarters to Belize
Head-quarters to Nassau
New Colours presented by Prince Alfred

1862 Quiah war
Capture of Magenbah
Capture of Majohn
Disbandment of the Sierra Leone Militia
Raising of the 4th West India Regiment
Gold Coast Artillery disbanded
Fifth West India Regiment raised

1863	Four companies move from Africa to West Indies Head-quarters move from Nassau to Barbados Distribution of regiment Nos. 3 and 7 companies retained on Gold Coast for service
1864	Second Ashanti War, return of 3 and 7 companies to West Indies Companies named by letters instead of numbers Distribution of regiment
1865	Jamaica Rebellion Move of Head-quarters from Barbados to Jamaica
1866	Change of distribution of regiment Left Wing to Gold Coast Head-quarters to Nassau Disturbance at Mumford Egbas threaten
1867	Gold Coast disturbance (Pram Pram)
1868	Colonel William Hill to command Colonel Whitfeild leaves the regiment
1869	Disbandment 4th West India Regiment, " I " company added to regiment Head-quarters from Nassau to Barbados Distribution of regiment
1870	3rd West India disbanded West Indies and West Africa distribution Lieut.-Colonel Harley retires Lieut.-Colonel Wise to command
1873	Ashanti War Engagement at Elmina Head-quarters to Africa Engagement at Essarman Action of Asianchi Reconnaissance from Dunquah Lieut.-Colonel Webber takes over command Action of Abra Crampa Tazoo Rear Guard Action Privates Fagan and Lewis's plucky reconnaissance

1874 Prah
Cross the Prah
Cross the Adansi
Insarfu
Quarman
Amoaful
Fall of Coomassie
Return march to the coast
Farewell General Orders
Regiment embarked for Sierra Leone
Names of officers served in campaign
Sails for West Indies
Head-quarters arrived at Jamaica
Address of Welcome (Jamaica)
Rewards, Ashanti
Distribution of Regiment
Issue of Ashanti medals

1875 Fire in Kingston (Jamaica)

1877 Head-quarters and six companies to Africa
West Africa and West Indies, Distribution

1878 Colonel Webber, half-pay
New Colours
Lieut.-Col. Brett appointed to command
Martini-Henry rifle issued

1879 Old Colours deposited at the Pro Cathedral, Demerara
Move to West Indies

1880 Distribution of regiment

1881 Ashanti scare, Cape Coast
Complimentary letter from O.C. Troops
Casualties
Barbados yellow fever outbreak

1882 Colonel Brett placed on half-pay
Colonel Sir W. O. Lanyon appointed to command
Great fire at Kingston
Wreck of s.s. "*Bolivar*"

1882	Head-quarters move to Barbados
	Detachment of three companies to West Coast Africa
	Lieut-Colonel Sheppard to command
1883	Head-quarters move to Africa
	Sherbo Expedition
	Letter from Horse Guards
	Letter from War Office
	Letter from Colonial Office
	Move from Africa to West Indies
	Distribution of regiment
1886	Inspection by Major-General Pearson
1887	Colonel Sheppard to half-pay
	Lieut-Colonel Talbot appointed to command
	Concentration of troops in West Indies
	Queen's Jubilee
	Colonel Talbot retires
	Lieut.-Colonel Patchett appointed to command
1888	Withdrawal from Honduras
	Amalgamation of 1st and 2nd West India Regiment
	Move to Africa
	Distribution of battalion
1890	Lieutenant Lendy, D.S.O.
1891	Cape Coast withdrawal
	Demerara, Detachment to St. Lucia
	Lieut.-Colonel Patchett to half-pay
	Lieut.-Colonel Maltby appointed to command
	Detachments to Gambia
1892	Expedition against Fodey Cabbah
	War medal granted
	Battalion to West Indies
	Lieut.-Colonel Maltby retires
	Lieut.-Colonel Caulfeild to command
	General's Inspection
1893	General's Inspection
	Old Colours at Demerara
	Battalion joined A.R. Association
	Issue of medals for Gambia

Subscribers towards cost of publication.

General CHAMBERLAYNE.
,, DRURY.
Major-General TALBOT.
Colonel BRETT.
Lt.-Col. MALTBY.
,, CAULFEILD-STOKER.
,, BAYLEY.
,, GORDON-GRANT.
,, LOVERIDGE.
,, ALLEN.
,, EGERTON.
,, BOURKE, D.S.O.
,, SEAFIELD GRANT.
Major DAVIES.
,, RYDE.
,, LOSCOMBE.
,, MINCHIN.
,, COOPER.
,, LOVEBAND.
,, MORGAN.
,, HENSTOCK.
,, BUCK.
,, DALRYMPLE-HAY.
,, STANSFELD.
,, SHERWOOD.
,, CROFTS.
,, DESBARRES.
,, LYSAGHT.
,, LOWRY.
,, BLACKDEN.
,, CARRE-SMITH.
Captain MOON.
,, SLESSOR.
,, WALTER.
,, CLIMO.
,, HARDYMAN.
,, ALONE.

Captain WOODMAN.
,, BLISS.
,, BARCHARD.
,, CRANE.
,, LEES.
,, CARLETON.
,, REW.
,, LITCHFORD.
,, THORNE.
,, SAUNDERS-DAVIES.
,, WAINRIGHT.
,, TICKELL.
,, MASTER.
,, MORLEY.
,, MCPHERSON.
,, DUNLOP.
,, WILSON.
,, LUARD.
,, BRIGHT-SMITH.
,, KENNA, V.C.
Lieut. MARTIN.
,, PEACOCKE.
,, LYNCH BLOSSE.
,, MURISON.
,, PRIDEAUX.
,, SWABY.
,, MARLEY.
,, BEADON.
,, DENHAM.
,, LEVERSON.
,, CHILL.
,, AMOS.
,, RUSSELL.
,, FITZMAURICE.
2nd ,, HILLS.
,, GIBB.
,, CAMERON.

FORSTER GROOM AND CO.,
MILITARY PUBLISHERS,
15, CHARING CROSS, S.W.